Advance Praise for *The Power of Ritual*

"If you are passionate about community building or simply seeking what feels good in life and how to get more of it . . . consider this book your new bible."

> —Cleo Wade, author of *Heart Talk* and *Where to Begin*

"*The Power of Ritual* is essential reading for anyone interested in how to find meaning in our strange, new world. Bursting with wisdom and compassion, this is the rare book that really might change your life. It has certainly changed mine."

> —John Green, author of *The Fault in Our Stars*

"Casper ter Kuile continues to have his pulse on this generation's search for meaning. Building on the incredible work of *How We Gather*, *The Power of Ritual* offers a radical proposition: we decide what's sacred."

> —Priya Parker, author of *The Art of Gathering*

"Casper ter Kuile's book is genuinely wise and utterly useful: it offers you the opportunity to remake your life in small but vital ways that will leave you happier, calmer, and more able to do the work that must be done on this planet. A classic the day it is published!"

> —Bill McKibben, author of *Radio Free Vermont*

"I've been waiting for a book like this. *The Power of Ritual* teaches us how to treat reading as sacred, fitness as sacred, alone time as sacred, and people as sacred. No blasphemy, but this book is my new sacred text!"

—Scott Heiferman, cofounder of Meetup

"Casper so perfectly captures the power of ritual in this very research-based, thought-provoking book. Ritual is an integral part of architecting community, and he thoroughly shares so many important examples of just how to integrate it in everyday life and in creating community. A must read for any leader."

—Radha Agrawal, cofounder and CEO of Daybreaker
and author of *Belong*

"As we reimagine our relationships with self, one another, and nature, *The Power of Ritual* provides deep insight into traditions both new and old. Brilliant."

—Elizabeth Cutler, cofounder of SoulCycle

"Human beings are made to experience the transcendent—for worship and, though this might surprise many people, for ritual as well. Casper ter Kuile invites our increasingly secular world to discover the sacred in the midst of the everyday and turn our days into rituals of joy, praise, and gratitude."

—James Martin, SJ, author of *The Jesuit Guide to (Almost) Everything* and *Jesus: A Pilgrimage*

The Power of Ritual

The Power of Ritual

TURNING EVERYDAY ACTIVITIES
INTO SOULFUL PRACTICES

Casper ter Kuile

HarperOne

An Imprint of HarperCollinsPublishers

HarperOne

HarperCollins books may be purchased for educational, business, or sales promotional use. For information, please email the Special Markets Department at SPsales@harpercollins.com.

FIRST EDITION

Designed by Terry McGrath

Library of Congress Cataloging-in-Publication Data

Names: Kuile, Casper ter, author.
Title: The power of ritual : turning everyday activities into soulful
   practices / Casper ter Kuile.
Description: New York, NY : HarperOne, 2020
Identifiers: LCCN 2019030898 (print) | LCCN 2019030899 (ebook) | ISBN
   9780062881816 (hardcover) | ISBN 9780062982810 | ISBN 9780062883537 |
   ISBN 9780062882066 (ebook)
Subjects: LCSH: Ritual. | Spiritual life.
Classification: LCC BL600 .K85 2020 (print) | LCC BL600 (ebook) | DDC
   390—dc23
LC record available at https://lccn.loc.gov/2019030898
LC ebook record available at https://lccn.loc.gov/2019030899

20 21 22 23 24   LSC   10 9 8 7 6 5 4 3 2 1

To my father, who taught me
when to follow the rules,
and my mother, who taught me
how to change them.

CONTENTS

Preface by Dacher Keltner ix

Introduction: The Paradigm Shift 1

1 Connecting with Self 31

2 Connecting with Others 81

3 Connecting with Nature 113

4 Connecting with Transcendence 151

5 Already Connected 185

Acknowledgments 201

PREFACE

W E LIVE IN AN ERA of fragmentation. Scholars have studied how our communities—families, churches, neighborhoods, work teams, and bowling leagues—are transforming. Once stable and enduring, now, as a result of economic and social forces, they are filled with people who have a more transient commitment to their jobs, locales, friendships, and marriages.

For deep and historical reasons, our sense of identity is now more fragmented, for better and worse. We have more complex and richer spiritual identities than in the past, more complex and richer gender identities, and more complex and richer ethnic identities. We are living in a globalized world.

There is much to praise in this era of fragmentation: the rise of rights and freedoms, the growing number of women in power, the democratization of art forms and information, and the glacial but accelerating move away from the homophobia, sexism, and racism that defined our recent history of colonial conquest.

But there is much to be concerned about, as well. People feel the absence of community. Studies find that the average citizen of the US, and likely the world, is lonelier than ever before. People have fewer friends. They spend inordinate amounts of time commuting in the car or scrolling through online feeds. People feel less trust toward their fellow citizens and work harder than before. The technologies many of us greeted with such enthusiasm a decade ago are now proving not to be the utopian, digital new world of connecting and sharing but a different kind of new world defined by anxiety, loneliness, endlessly comparing oneself to others, and perhaps surveillance. Our era of fragmentation has paved the way for an era of anxiety.

And this fragmentation has pronounced costs for the mind and body. As a professor of psychology, I teach the science of happiness at University of California, Berkeley, and beyond to hundreds of thousands of people in online courses, digital content, and my podcast, *The Science of Happiness.* Over the twenty years of this engagement, I have been asked one key question: How might I find deeper happiness?

The science points to an answer in the abstract: Find more community. Deepen your connections with others. Be with others in meaningful ways. Find rituals to organize your life. It will boost your happiness, give you greater joy, and even add ten years to your life expectancy, science suggests. Deep connections and the sense of community reduce levels of stress-related cortisol; they activate reward and safety circuits in the brain; they activate a region of the nervous system called the vagus nerve, which slows down our cardiovascular system and opens us up to others; and they lead to the release of oxytocin, a neurochemical that promotes cooperation, trust, and generosity. But I have been hard-pressed to point to deep, practical, principled ways to build connection, community, and a sense of ritual.

Now I can. In Casper ter Kuile's illuminating book *The Power of Ritual: Turning Everyday Activities into Soulful Practices*, we find a road map to greater meaning in life through community. A first step is through the creation of everyday secular rituals. Rituals, in my view, are patterned, repeated ways in which we enact the moral emotions—of compassion, gratitude, awe, bliss, empathy, ecstasy—that have been shaped by our hominid evolution and built up into the fabric of our culture through cultural evolution. I learned this from Casper during the summer of 2018. He invited me into a ritualized experience of Saint-Germain-des-Prés, my favorite cathedral in Paris. Before entering the illuminated space inside, we circled around the building, clockwise, taking in the stream of sounds and images that meditative walking brings about. We then offered alms to a man begging at the entrance feeling the deep sympathies of charity. Before sitting in a pew, we genuflected and made a request and offered a quiet reflective thought—prayer—for someone we care for. We took in the stained-glass windows and their patterns and colors, so reflective of the patterns and beauty of nature—veins in leaves, colors of trees, reflections on lakes. Our attention moved up to the apse of the cathedral as though looking up to the clouds in the sky. We crossed ourselves in an act of quiet touch. Although I am not religious, these simple acts of ritual—like those that run through this book—brought me a feeling of calm, reverence, and even grace.

Rituals create patterns of the greatest capacities that I believe were given to us in the process of evolution and elaborated upon in our cultural evolution: our capacity to share, to sing, to chant, to revere, to find beauty, to dance, to imagine, to quietly reflect, and to sense something beyond what we see. Casper's book points to higher-order principles through which you can create more ritual in your fragmented life. Read sacred texts (this past June I reread Walt Whitman's "Song of Myself," a sacred text in my family, and was moved again). Create sabbaths in your life, from work, technology, social life, and our frenetic, often overscheduled hours of the day. Find opportunities for what one might call prayer—mindful quiet forms of reflecting on love, gratitude, and contrition. Eat with others. Seek out nature, that universal source of transcending the self, that so often repairs, as Emerson observed, "life's calamities." In the spirit of our fragmented lives, Casper encourages us, through his broad, synthetic view of spiritual life, to weave together a fabric of rituals to bring meaning and community to our lives.

Casper offers perhaps a more challenging prospect, too: to awaken to the ritual and community that you are already in-

stinctively creating in your social life. We have a biological
need to belong, scientists have shown; without community,
as in solitary confinement, we lose our minds. We seek out
and create rituals with alacrity and force. For twenty years, I
played pickup basketball until I depleted the cartilage in my
knees. I played in nearly every city I visited, from Santa Monica, California, to Brockton, Massachusetts, to cities in France.
I played with anyone. I was not even that skilled a player. And
when I had to hang up my high-tops, what I missed most was
not points scored or victories eked out, but the rituals that
hold people together in pickup basketball: fist bumps, forms of
protest and contrition, celebration and dance, ritualized patterns of five people moving together on a basketball court. It
is sublime.

Casper's brilliant book challenges us to see and feel the rituals that are already part of our lives, to switch our minds
to a community mind-set. It is likely happening in your spin
class, on climbing trips, at musical concerts, when you shop
for food, as you dine with your family, in the patterns of play,
conversation, and celebrating and consoling on children's soccer fields—and even in how you might use your smartphone,
in its better moments, to share photos, recipes, quotes, jokes,
GIFs, memes, and news. After reading *The Power of Ritual*, I
came to see how much ritual already ran through my daily
life. And I felt lifted up.

Social, economic, and architectural forces, such as the rise
of single-family housing, have made this an era of fragmentation. There is much to decry about that, and we feel it in the

pains of isolation and loneliness. But there is much freedom and promise in this fragmentation, to create community and ritual in a richer and more complex fashion, one that honors and celebrates the diversity that is our species. *The Power of Ritual* points us toward this promise.

Dacher Keltner
Professor of Psychology, UC Berkeley
Faculty Director, Greater Good Science Center

The Paradigm Shift

As a teenager, I was convinced: *You've Got Mail* was the greatest movie of all time.

Kathleen Kelly and Joe Fox, played by Meg Ryan and Tom Hanks, meet online in the early days of AOL chat rooms. (We're in 1998 here—think Monica's "The Boy Is Mine" and Bill Clinton's sex scandal.) All they know about each other is that they love books and they love New York City—nothing else. Not even one another's real name. And through the back-and-forth emails that they send each other, they fall in love. They're honest with each other about their secret fears and hopes and pain. They share everything that they don't tell even their partners. This is the best of online anonymity—feeling intimately connected and totally safe at the same time.

And connected and safe were two things I didn't feel at all.

I was a gay kid living in an English boarding school with fifty testosterone-fueled teenage boys. I stuck out like a sore thumb. A look around my bedroom, shared with three others, revealed all you needed to know. As you walked in there were posters of half-naked supermodels and racing cars to the right, pictures of the band Slipknot in their horror masks to the left, and then in my corner, a complete collection of Agatha Christie books and glitter gel pens.

Needless to say, I wasn't the first boy chosen for the rugby team. Or the soccer team. Or anything, really. (I did join an aerobics class, breaking boundaries for all future queer kids in the school, I hope, but that's another story.)

I felt lonely all the time. I would go on walks and pretend I was a hairdresser asking myself out loud about any vacations I was going on. I tried to ingratiate myself with the older boys by making them toasted Nutella sandwiches like a baboon trying to demonstrate submission on the savanna—please don't hurt me, I will bring you food!

So, you can imagine why a movie about love and connection and joy meant so much to me. And it's important to say that (spoiler ahead) the two characters in *You've Got Mail* don't actually meet until the final—my least favorite—scene. The movie is about the *promise* of love and connection, more than the actual experience of it. I longed for that kind of connection. And a tiny part of me trusted the universe enough to know that perhaps, one day, ideally in glamorous Manhattan, I might find my own version of a literary multimillionaire who had a dog called Brinkley.

I've re-watched *You've Got Mail* many, many times. But it represents so much more to me than just a movie now, because I've made it more meaningful. I have very specific rituals for when and how to watch (always alone, always with a tub of Pralines and Cream Häagen Dazs ice cream). It's not an "Oh, what shall we watch?" kind of movie; it's an "I'm feeling lost and alone, and I need everything I've got to bring me out of this slump" kind of movie. Certain lines are inscribed on my heart, like mantras. Characters are totems of how I want to be—or not be—in the world. While for most people it's just another rom-com, for me, *You've Got Mail* is sacred.

That's what this book is all about—taking things we do every day and layering meaning and ritual onto them, even experiences as ordinary as reading or eating—by thinking of them as spiritual practices. After more than half a decade of research and thousands of conversations with people around the country, I am convinced that we are in the midst of a paradigm shift. That what used to hold us in community no longer works. That the spiritual offerings of yesteryear no longer help us thrive. And that, just like stargazers of the sixteenth century had to reimagine the cosmos by placing the sun at the center of the solar system, so we need to fundamentally rethink what it means for something to be sacred. Paradigm shifts like this happen for two reasons. First, because there is new evidence that refutes previously held assumptions—think of how Charles Darwin's *Origin of Species* transformed our understanding of evolutionary biology and the historical accuracy of the Bible, for example. Second, because older theories prove irrelevant to new questions that people start asking. And that's what is happening today. In this time of rapid religious and relational change, a new landscape of meaning-making and community is emerging—and the traditional structures of spirituality are struggling to keep up with what our lives look like.

I've written this book to help you recognize the practices of connection that you already have: the habits and traditions already in your bones that can deepen your experience of meaning, reflection, sanctuary, and joy—perhaps at a yoga class, or by reading your favorite books, looking at the setting sun, making art, or lighting candles. It might be through lifting weights, hiking nature trails, meditating, or dancing and singing with others. Whatever it is, we'll start there by affirming those things as worthy of our attention, and we'll notice how they make up a broader cultural shift in how we build connection to what matters most.

Religious traditions that were supposed to serve us have often failed. Worse, many have actively excluded us. So we need to find a new way forward. Drawing on the best of what has come before, we can find ourselves in the emerging story of what it means to live deeply connected. Even without espousing specific religious beliefs, the practices that we'll explore in this book, whether daily rituals or annual traditions, can collectively form our contemporary spiritual life. These gifts and their wisdom have been passed on through generations. Now it's our turn to interpret them. Here and now. You and me.

I'm so glad we're in this together.

"CROSSFIT IS MY CHURCH"

I have spent the last seven years exploring the idea that just because people are leaving church doesn't mean that they're less spiritual. As a ministry innovation fellow at Harvard Divinity School, I've studied the changing landscape of American religion with my colleague Angie Thurston. We published *How We Gather,** a paper documenting how people are building communities of meaning in secular spaces, in essence performing the functions historically handled by traditional religious institutions. That paper has been praised by bishops and the former CEO of Twitter alike, as we've had the joy of mapping and connecting with America's most innovative community leaders and meaning-makers.

Through hundreds of interviews and site visits and lots of reading, Angie and I kept track of secular communities that seemed to be doing religious things. Wherever we went and whoever we spoke to, it became our habit to ask, "So where do you go to find community?"

Time and again, the answers surprised us. November Project. Groupmuse. Cosecha. Tough Mudder. Camp Grounded. But the one that really threw me was CrossFit.

People didn't just talk about it as their community. "CrossFit is my church" became the refrain. When we interviewed then Harvard Business School student Ali Huberlie, she said, "My CrossFit box [gym] is everything to me. I've met my boy-

---

* *How We Gather*, https://sacred.design/insights.

friend and some of my very best friends through CrossFit. . . . When [we] started apartment hunting this spring, we immediately zeroed in on the neighborhood closest to our [CrossFit] box—even though it would increase our commute to work. We did this because we couldn't bear to leave our community. At our box, we have babies and little kids crawling around everywhere, and it has been an amazing experience to watch those little ones grow up."

"CrossFit is family, laughter, love, and community. I can't imagine my life without the people I've met through it." At Ali's gym, or box as it's called in the CrossFit world, people gather on Friday night for drinks as well as five or six times a week to work out together. Across town at another affiliate box, there's an expecting mothers' group, and the box hosts a talent night where members try out stand-up comedy or play the cello for the first time in twenty years.

Cofounder Greg Glassman never set out to build a community, but he's embraced the role of quasi-spiritual leader with open arms. In an interview with us at Harvard Divinity School, he explained, "We kept being asked 'Are you a cult?' And after a while I realized, maybe we are. This is an active, sweating, loving, breathing community. It's not an insult to a CrossFitter to be called part of a cult. Discipline, honesty, courage, accountability—what you learn in the gym is also training for life. CrossFit makes better people." His remarks at times sound outright religious. "We're the stewards of something," he said. Even though CrossFit is a privately owned corporation, he thinks of his leadership role as distinctly priestly—he talks about "shepherding a flock" and "tending an orchard" of CrossFit boxes. And the flock responds—they call him simply Coach.

Perhaps this shouldn't have surprised us. After all, CrossFit is famous for its evangelical proselytizing. In applying to open a box, trainers are required to attend a two-day seminar and write an essay about why they want to open a box. What HQ looks for in these essays is not an applicant's business savvy, training skills, or fitness level—the key ingredient is whether one's life has been changed by CrossFit and whether the applicant wants to change other people's lives with CrossFit. It's that simple. (Compare that to five years of rabbinical study or three years of divinity school!) The evangelical tone is not just about getting a hot body—the mission is much bigger. CrossFit is a lifesaving strategy, according to Coach Greg. "Three hundred fifty thousand Americans are going to die next year from sitting on the couch. That's dangerous. The TV is dangerous. Squatting isn't." Particularly, Glassman is at war with America's soda industry. As diabetes rates continue to climb and Coca-Cola and PepsiCo fund public health research that minimizes the impact of a high-calorie diet, Glassman sees Big Soda as the next frontier of corporate crime. Indeed, CrossFit is becoming ever more civically involved. In Southern California, gym leaders invited a local politician to hold rallies in their communities, joining forces to take on the Big Soda lobby. Nationally, CrossFit is also affiliated with a network of nonprofit gyms supporting people in their recovery journey from addiction.

Even more striking, and much like religious congregations, CrossFit has found a way to honor its dead—specifically, members who have died in the line of fire: military service members, police officers, and firefighters. And it isn't simply naming them; their memories are embodied in the combination of burpees, lifts, and pull-ups that make up a Workout of the Day that the CrossFit faithful practice around the world. Former CrossFit television host Rory Mckernan introduced a workout named "the Josie" in honor of Deputy US Marshal Josie Wells who died as he attempted to serve an arrest warrant on a double-murder suspect in Baton Rouge, Louisiana. Mckernan introduces the hero workout in a video by saying, "Speak his name. Understand what he did. Think about giving your life in the service of something greater than yourself and what that means for those left behind. And do that before you do the workout. I promise you that it will alter the way you attack it. Rest in peace, my friend."

With over fifteen thousand communities worldwide, this phenomenon was something Angie and I had to pay attention to. And even though people new to CrossFit often came to lose weight or build muscle, what kept them coming back was the deeply engaged and committed community.

CrossFit was the most surprising and widespread example of people building community that echoed religious traditions, but it wasn't the only one. Other fitness communities like Tough Mudder had similar qualities. At Tough Mudder, a community of people who get together to overcome a complex obstacle course—usually covered in mud—the leadership is wholly unafraid of religious comparisons. Founder Will Dean explained to Fast Company in 2017 that Tough Mudder races are "the pilgrimage, the big, annual festivals, like Christmas and Easter. But then we also have the gym, which becomes the local church, the community gathering hub. You have the media, which is a little like praying. Then there's the apparel, which is a little like wearing your cross or your headscarf or any other form of religious apparel."

Yet fitness communities aren't the only way that people are finding and exploring questions of belonging. Groups that gather people around play and the creative arts were also spaces for building community. At Artisan's Asylum, a maker space in Somerville, Massachusetts, a community has formed of artists, artisans, tinkerers, jewelry makers, robot creators, captains of mutant bicycles that look like space-ships, engineers, designers, and more. The creative spirit that runs through the space is embodied in the generosity of members showing one another how to use unfamiliar machines or materials. An active mailing list helps source difficult-to-find parts and helps new artisans get started. One woman shared that she wanted to make a complex but-terfly Halloween costume for her young daughter involving lights that would flash on and off. Within hours, the mate-rial she needed had arrived on her doorstep and a highly skilled maker was ready to guide her through the process. At Thanksgiving, the whole community gathers for a giant potluck they call Makersgiving, with their creations adorn-ing the long tables alongside homemade dishes. But Artisan's

Asylum has become more than a community. It is the place where people come to grow into the person they want to be. Learning a new skill like welding gives members the confidence to try something new like improv or singing. Becoming a mentor to someone new to a craft shapes how members see themselves in the world. And because the space is open twenty-four hours a day, and a number of members have insecure housing, the whole community has become passionate about advocating to city government about better public housing. The congregational parallels are not difficult to spot.

After a year and a half of interviews and participant observation, Angie and I were ready to share what we'd learned in our *How We Gather* paper. We found that not only did secular spaces offer people connection in similar ways that religious institutions once did, but they also provided other things that filled a spiritual purpose. Communities that we studied offered people opportunities for personal and social transformation, offered a chance to be creative and clarify their purpose, and provided structures of accountability and community connection.

And because the leaders of these communities became trusted and respected, they were often approached by community members about life's biggest questions and transitions. We heard of weddings and funerals being led by yoga instructors and art class teachers, of people being counseled through a diagnosis or breakup by leaders more expert in fitness than finer matters of the heart and spirit. One SoulCycle instructor remembered getting a text on a Sunday afternoon from one of her regular riders simply asking, "Should I divorce my husband?" With no formal training or preparation to handle these momentous life transitions, community leaders did their best anyway. Communities rallied around members who were sick–bringing food, raising money for hospital visits, and driving them to appointments. More and more, even though they looked nothing like traditional congregations, we saw how old patterns of community were finding new expressions in a contemporary context.

What studying these modern communities taught me is this: we are building lives of meaning and connection outside of traditional religious spaces, but making it up as we go along can only take us so far. We need help to ground and enrich those practices. And if we are brave enough to look, it is in the ancient traditions where we find incredible insight and creativity that we can adapt for our modern world.

Why This Matters

Noticing these shifts in community behavior isn't just interesting. It's important. In the midst of a crisis of isolation, where loneliness leads to deaths of despair, being truly connected isn't a luxury. It's a lifesaver.

Rates of social isolation are rocketing sky-high. More and more of us are lonely and unable to connect with others in the way that we long to. A 2006 paper in the *American Socio-*

logical Review documented how the average number of people that Americans say they can talk to about important things declined from 2.94 in 1985 to 2.08 in 2004. Essentially, we've each lost someone to care for us in the moments when we most need it—and that number includes family members and spouses as well as friends. Our social fabric is fraying.

Health officials now talk of social isolation as an epidemic. When Dr. Vivek Murthy moved through his confirmation process to become the nineteenth US Surgeon General in 2014, he was asked which health issues he particularly hoped to address. In an interview with Quartz, he explained that he "didn't list loneliness in that priority list because it was not one at the time." But while traveling around the country, he met numerous people who would tell him stories of their struggles with addiction and violence, with chronic illnesses like diabetes, and with mental illnesses like anxiety and depression. Whatever the issue, social isolation made it worse. "What was often unsaid were these stories of loneliness, which would take time to come out. They would not say, 'Hello, I am John Q, I am lonely.' What they said was 'I have been struggling with this illness, or my family is struggling with this problem,' and when I would dig a bit it would come out." Disconnection sours the sweet things in life and makes any hardship nearly unbearable. Indeed, suicide rates are at a thirty-year high.

The data are clear. In a landmark meta-analysis of over seventy studies, Dr. Julianne Holt-Lunstad demonstrated that social isolation is more harmful to our health than smoking fifteen cigarettes a day or being obese. Holt-Lunstad concludes in her 2018 *American Psychologist* paper that "there are perhaps no other facets that can have such a large impact on both length and quality of life—from the cradle to the grave" as social connection.

While our culture often lifts up the importance of self-care, we're desperately in need of community care. Without it, the impact of social isolation shows up in numerous ways. It is harder to find work. We fall out of healthy habits. And in heat waves or superstorms, we're more likely to be forgotten by neighbors and perish.

Perversely, when we feel far away from one another, our brains have evolved not to foster connection, but instead to strive for self-preservation. Vulnerability and empathy expert Dr. Brené Brown explains in her book *Braving the Wilderness*, "When we feel isolated, disconnected, and lonely, we try to protect ourselves. In that mode, we want to connect, but our brain is attempting to override connection with self-protection. That means less empathy, more defensiveness, more numbing, and less sleeping. . . . Unchecked loneliness fuels continued loneliness by keeping us afraid to reach out." My husband and I call this entering the doom spiral, where one thing leads to another, and soon it feels impossible to get out.

Once in the doom spiral, our brains desperately try to counteract the loss of social connection but struggle to do this alone. In his landmark book *In Over Our Heads*, Harvard developmental psychologist Dr. Robert Kegan explains, "The mental

burden of modern life may be nothing less than the extraor-
dinary cultural demand that each person, in adulthood, create
internally an order of consciousness comparable to that which
ordinarily would only be found at the level of a community's
collective intelligence." More simply put, we need to recreate
an entire village network of support in our own brain. Alone.
And this goes far beyond physical support and even mental
health. "We feel unaccompanied at the level of our own souls,"
writes Kegan.

Yet despite the dire warnings that these statistics offer,
there is hope. The solutions are age-old and all around us. As
much as for our joy as for our health, we can deepen our existing connections to the world around us and to one another.
We can regrow those relationships that have withered away.
We can be one another's medicine.

I have learned that disconnection is about more than
our physical and emotional well-being. Our spirits, too, suffer. Without rich relationships and a sense of connection to
something bigger than ourselves, the occasions that could
mean the most in our lives feel emptier. As we encounter major life moments—weddings, births, funerals—we often find
ourselves at a loss for how to mark them without the rituals
we once had with religion. Think of Cheryl Strayed's story
in her memoir, *Wild*, about how, without a religious upbring-
ing, she didn't know what to do when her mother died. What
would happen at the funeral? Who could she go to for help
during her grief? Generations before us turned to the church
or the temple during these times: the priest or rabbi would

lead the funeral ceremony, congregation members organized meal deliveries for the family, and everything was taken care of. All of us would know what to do. But today? Just like Strayed, we're overwhelmed. Without clarity on what to do when we meet these milestones, we let them pass by, unable to live through them wholeheartedly.

More than that, the number of occasions we deem worthy of ritual are embarrassingly small. It strikes me that as the cost and stress of weddings has gone up, the number of other rituals and celebrations has gone down. If we no longer celebrate spring or harvest time, the new moon or a young person's coming-of-age, is it any wonder that our human hunger for meaning gets amped up on the one day *in our lives* when we're actively engaged with designing a ceremonial experience?

What I propose is this: by composting old rituals to meet our real-world needs, we can regrow deeper relationships and speak to our hunger for meaning and depth.

But why are we in this mess? We need to understand the era-defining patterns in religious decline that we're in, and what that decline means for each of our lives.

RISE OF THE "NONES"

Much has been written about the decline of religion and the rise of the so-called "nones" (people who tick "None of the above" when asked about their religious identity). Whereas nearly a century ago, Americans could assume that just about everyone around them fit into a religious box—Catholic, Presbyterian, Reform Jewish, AME, Quaker—today, many of us straddle multiple identities or have none at all. Perhaps you grew up with a Hindu father and a Jewish mother, celebrated both Passover and Dewali, and now find yourself practicing a bit of both. Or your former-Methodist parents took you to an Episcopal Sunday school for a few years before church slowly drifted into the background of family life. Or perhaps, like me, you weren't raised with anything in particular, but celebrated popular holidays and had a mix of family rituals and traditions. Wherever you fall on this spectrum, you are part of the shifting sands of religious identity and practice. The percentage of Americans who describe themselves as atheist, agnostic, or "nothing in particular" has grown to 26 percent, and 2019 General Social Survey data suggests that nones are now as numerous as evangelicals and Catholics in the United States.

Unsurprisingly, the trend is most pronounced for young people. Among millennials (those born between 1980 and 1995), the number stands at 40 percent, according to a Pew Research Center poll published in 2019. Research data also suggests that each new generation is less religious than the last. A Barna Group poll in 2018 revealed that 13 percent of Gen Zers consider themselves atheists, more than double the 6 percent of American adults overall. But the trend toward disaffiliation holds true across every age cohort. In 2014, nearly one in five boomers were nones (17 percent), and nearly

one in four Gen Xers fit the same bill (23 percent). All this results in massive changes in our religious infrastructure. For
instance, Mark Chaves, a sociologist at Duke University, has
estimated that over three-and-a-half thousand churches close
their doors every year.

America is not alone in these trends, of course. In Europe
it's an even starker picture. A 2017 survey by the British National Centre for Social Research revealed that 71 percent of
eighteen- to twenty-four-year-olds consider themselves as
nonreligious, while UK church attendance has declined from
nearly 12 percent to 5 percent between 1980 and 2015.

Again, this isn't to say that we are becoming less spiritual
per se. But the data does tell us that *how* we engage our spirituality is changing.

It may be helpful to think of the human longing that leads
to religious culture as akin to music and the music industry,
which has struggled mightily over the last twenty years, with
CD sales in free fall for much of the 2000s and 2010s. But our
love for music itself endures. Decades after the technology-
induced crisis, industry executives have figured out a new
business model—combining streaming subscriptions with vi-
nyl sales, which are at a fourteen-year high. The same thing is
happening in our spiritual lives: a mix of fast-paced innovation and rich tradition. Attendance at congregations is down,
but our hunger for community and meaning remains. Formal
affiliation is declining, but millions are downloading meditation apps and attending weekend retreats. Moreover, they find
spiritual lessons and joys in completely "nonreligious" places

like yoga classes, Cleo Wade and Rupi Kaur poetry, and accompaniment groups like Alcoholics Anonymous and the Dinner Party (a community-based grief support group for twenty- and thirtysomethings). Stadium concerts and karaoke replace congregational singing, and podcasts and tarot decks replace sermons or wisdom teachings.

In her book *Choosing Our Religion*, Elizabeth Drescher explains that we nones see our spiritual lives as organic and emerging, responding to the people around us rather than structured into dogmatic categories of belief and identity. Said otherwise, we're less likely to affiliate with an institution than we are to affiliate with another individual. We see religious institutions as being driven by hypocrisy and greed, judgmentalism and sexual abuse, anti-scientific ignorance and homophobia. People also leave religious communities behind because worship experiences are simply boring or formulaic. Most interesting to me is that we are especially wary of a religious identity that threatens to "overwrite [our] self-identity in ways that seem to compromise personal integrity and authenticity," as Drescher writes. All this makes us nervous to even acknowledge that we might have a spiritual life. Tellingly, over half of Drescher's hundred plus interviewees used the phrase "or whatever" whenever they talked about something spiritual in their own life!

So let me say this clearly. However you express your spiritual life, it is legitimate. If you touch the sacred on the basketball court or on the beach, in cooking or crafting, in snuggling with your dog or singing in a crowd of thousands, during Yom Kippur services or at an altar call, while you read these pages you never need to say "or whatever," okay? You can think of this book as giving you your dose of spiritual confidence and social permission.

Unbundling Traditions and Remixing Them

Like nearly everything else in contemporary culture, how we understand religion is shaped by the technological changes driving our lives, especially the rise of the internet. Institutions have lost our trust, particularly those that claim expertise and authority. But as Joi Ito, former director of the MIT Media Lab, explains in his book *Whiplash* coauthored with Jeff Howe, the emergent systems aren't replacing authority. Instead, what's changing is the basic attitude toward information. "The Internet has played a key role in this, providing a way for the masses not only to be heard, but to engage in the kind of discussion, deliberation, and coordination that just recently were the province of professional politics."[*]

Let's unpack that. The internet era has opened us to the possibility of curating and creating our own tailored practices and to looking to our peers for guidance as much as any teacher or authority figure. There are two key concepts here—unbundling and remixing.

Unbundling is the process of separating elements of value

---

[*] The irony is not lost on me that it was precisely Ito's lack of transparency that resulted in his departure from the Media Lab in 2019.

from a single collection of offerings. Think of a local newspaper. Whereas fifty years ago it provided classifieds, personal ads, letters to the editor, a puzzle for your commute, and of course the actual news, today its competitors have surpassed it in each of these, making the daily paper all but obsolete. Craigslist, Tinder, Facebook, HQ Trivia, and cable news offer more personalization, deeper engagement, and perfect immediacy. The newspaper has been unbundled, and end users mix together their own preferred set of services. Printed news is having to find a new value that it alone offers.

The same is true for our spiritual lives. Fifty years ago, most people in the United States relied on a single religious community to offer connection, conduct spiritual practices, ritualize life moments, foster healing, connect to lineage, inspire morality, house transcendent experience, mark holidays, support family, serve the needy, work for justice, and—through art, song, text, and speech—tell and retell a common story to bind them together. Further back, religious institutions provided health care and education too. Today, all of these offerings have become unbundled. Some health care and education is provided by the state, while for those who can afford it, various private corporations provide the rest. Communal seasonal celebrations have shifted to sporting events like the Super Bowl, national celebrations like the Fourth of July and Thanksgiving, with only a sprinkling of religious highlights remaining, most notably Christmas. As for life transition rituals? We mostly make those up with our friends as we go along, if we have enough time and energy for it.

We might introspect by using a meditation app like Head-space or Insight Timer, find ecstatic moments of connection at a Beyoncé concert, and go hiking to find calm and beauty. We set our intentions at spin classes and make a note of thanks in our gratitude journal. We express our connection to ancestors through the dishes we cook, we feel part of something bigger than us at a protest or a Pride parade. The core needs of intro-spection, ecstatic experience, beauty, feeling like we're part of something bigger—these have existed for millennia. But how we create these experiences varies over time. Where religious institutions have been mistaken, as innovation expert Clay-ton Christensen might put it, is that they've fallen in love with a specific solution, rather than forever evolving to meet the need.

Meanwhile, there's a growing number of mixed-religion households. Before the 1960s only 20 percent of married cou-ples were in interfaith unions, while in this century's first de-cade 45 percent were, according to journalist Naomi Schaefer Riley. Harvard Divinity School dean David Hempton labels this phenomenon "braiding." Jewish teacher Reb Zalman calls it "hy-phenating." Marketing guru Bob Moesta refers to it as "remixing." Whatever we call it, and however much religious institutions re-sist it, it is happening. And not just in the United States.

Anthropologist Satsuki Kawano describes how Japanese people have been Shintoists and Buddhists at the same time for decades, practicing elements of both traditions without seeing themselves as necessarily members of two separate re-ligions. In her book *Ritual Practice in Modern Japan*, she explains that the Japanese state has tried to separate the two religions but that, despite its efforts, the two remain deeply entwined. There have been tensions and conflicts through the decades, but no religious wars or effort to eliminate one another. Indeed, Shinto and Buddhist traditions have interacted, and whole theologies integrating the two have come to flourish. "As a result," she writes, "mutual influence [has] led to a complex orchestration and integration of native and indigenized foreign practices without completely eliminating distinctions between the two traditions." One might go to a Shinto shrine for weddings and children's celebrations but have one's funeral in a Buddhist temple, for example.

But as we benefit from unbundling and remixing traditions that allow us ever more personalization, we find that we share less and less with one another. We're left isolated and longing for connection.

FOUR LEVELS OF CONNECTION

Like me, you might have been raised without a religious background. Or perhaps you were born into an identity that doesn't quite fit. You might be atheist, agnostic, at the edge of your tradition(s), spiritual-but-not-religious, unsatisfied in your spiritual home, or simply unsure. Whatever language you use to describe yourself, you've been patching together your spiritual life and are longing for something authentic, something more meaningful, something deeper.

The purpose of this book is to show you how you can transform your daily habits into practices that create a sacred foundation for your life. I'll share some ancient tools reimagined for today's culture, and I'll tell some stories about others who are showing us a way forward.

Deep connection isn't just about relationships with other people. It's about feeling the fullness of being alive. It's about being enveloped in multiple layers of belonging within, between, and around us. This book is an invitation to deepen your rituals of connection across four levels:

- Connecting with yourself
- Connecting with the people around you
- Connecting with the natural world
- Connecting with the transcendent.*

Each layer of connection strengthens the other, so that when we feel deeply connected across those four levels, it's as if our days are held within a rich latticework of meaning. We're able to be kinder, more forgiving. We heal. We grow.

And each of these layers is rooted in insights from many of the world's wisdom traditions. For thousands of years those traditions have kept communities together, helped people grieve loss and celebrate joy. The great myths of the world helped us make moral sense out of chaos and catastrophe.

---

* I'm indebted to Sarah E. Koss and Mark D. Holder for their definition of spirituality as "a feeling of Connectedness to something greater than oneself, experienced through cultivating a relationship with oneself, one's community, one's environment, and one's perception of the transcendent," which, in part, inspired the structure of this book.

Even if we're a little nervous to engage the traditions, they have much to teach us.

Some things have changed, of course, since these ancient traditions were established. No longer do we need myths to explain how the sun rises and sets, where floods come from, and what lies underground. Instead we have new questions. How can we truly find rest in a stressed-out 24/7 world? How can we remember our "enough-ness" in an economy that always pushes for more? How do we cultivate our courage to stand against injustice?

In Chapter 1 I'll explore two everyday practices that help us connect to our authentic self: sacred reading and sabbath. Chapter 2 proposes eating and exercising together as two sacred tools to help us connect deeply with others. Chapter 3 focuses on reimagining pilgrimage and the liturgical calendar to connect us more intimately with the natural world, and Chapter 4 explores what connecting to the divine might look like by reframing prayer and participating in a regular small group of support and accountability. Finally, Chapter 5 is a reminder that we are all inherently born into belonging. The practices here are simply the tools to help us remember.

I've written this book because, although there is much practical guidance out there, it is often bundled up with bits of religious culture that are hard to decipher and painful to stomach. Institutions have turned mysteries into dogmas. They've lost the lightness of touch to translate timeless wisdom into relevant teaching. It is time to liberate the gifts of tradition so that all of us can live lives of integrity and joy.

Each of us has permission to curate and create rituals that will help us connect, and I hope these pages can be a source of accompaniment as you make your own way.

Throughout the book I'll share my own attempts as a spiritual beginner, some of which I hope can be of practical help for your own journey. I also hope this book will help us be less isolated in our spiritual lives. The interlocking systems of oppression depend on our feeling alone and ashamed. The gift of spiritual practices is that they cultivate courage, so that we will risk more for one another. Nothing would bring me greater happiness than knowing that sacred reading groups become hubs of activism, that learning the same songs means we can sing them together in the streets.

INTENTION, ATTENTION, AND REPETITION

Words like "spiritual practices" and "rituals" conjure up monks in dimly lit temples or extremely difficult yoga poses. (And they can be those things!) But what I mean follows the wisdom given to me by activist and minister Kathleen McTigue, who looks for three things in any practice or ritual: intention, attention, and repetition. So, though you may take the dog out for a walk numerous times a day, ticking off the repetition component, it isn't a ritual practice if you're also on the phone because you're not really paying attention to your pup and the walk you're on. It's simply a habit. Or, you might read every night before bedtime, but not really bring any specific intention to it. Again, that doesn't match our description of a ritual or practice.

However, I've come to believe that just about anything can *become* a spiritual practice—gardening, painting, singing, snuggling, sitting. The world is full of these rituals! Just look at the pregame handshakes at a Cleveland Cavaliers basketball game. We just need to be clear about our intention (what are we inviting into this moment?), bring it our attention (coming back to being present in this moment), and make space for repetition (coming back to this practice time and again). In this way, rituals make the invisible connections that make life meaningful, visible.

If you're like me, you'll try out lots of different things that don't quite vibe or fall away after a couple of tries. That's absolutely fine. If, after some time, you find one or two things that start to feel consistently like they're *your* practices, that's when you've got a winner.

A Note on That Word "Spiritual"

It is easy to avoid the "spiritual" today. We try to satiate our longing for connection by scrolling endlessly through social media feeds. My personal favorite is the YouTube hole, where after an hour I look up from my phone and can't believe the time that's passed while I've been watching drag queens or soccer match recaps.

When we do pay attention to the moments of real meaning, they can overwhelm us. Holding a baby in our arms for the first time, hearing music that makes us weep, being out on the water and feeling completely at one with the elements around us—it can be overpowering to feel deeply connected. These moments unlock memories, longings, traumas, and frequently, tears. And to me, these moments are sacred. They are spiritual. But usually, we allow time to pass, and these moments drift away. The shimmering flashes of life's fullness get lost behind the stack of unanswered email and the relentless drudgery of the everyday. We forget the intention we'd set to go out into the forest more often, to start making music again, to spend more time with the ones we love. (At least I know I do.)

Think about your own life. When was the last time you felt deeply connected to something bigger than yourself? Where were you? What did that feel like? And what words would you use to communicate that experience? By and large, we are starved of good language to describe what matters most to us, to confidently communicate with others those moments of deep meaning. And as spiritual teacher, scholar, and activist Barbara Holmes writes, our isolation in experiencing moments like these further privatizes our interpretation of them. Neuroscience, too, tells us that when we can't fully describe what we're feeling, we tend to discount the feeling itself as illegitimate or unworthy of our—or other's—attention.

Stay with me if you can, even if these words feel a little uncomfortable. Imagine they're beautiful new leather shoes that are still a little rigid as you walk. They just need some time before they've molded to the shape of your feet. Soon enough you'll have found the right words, or become used to these, to help you pinpoint that feeling we're talking about together.

This language challenge isn't random. It's tricky for a reason. We've been taught to see the world as divided between
the sacred and the profane, the religious and the secular. We've
been taught that there's somehow a line that makes a church
building sacred and a supermarket secular. That vertical line
is an invention. Instead, imagine a horizontal line between
the shallow and the deep. It stretches across every place and
every person. When we can sink below the blur of habit, we
can be present to that portion of our experience where we find
deepest meaning. Maybe it's poetry that takes us there. Or an
incredible piece of theater. Or psychedelics. Or the arms of our
beloved. Or simply watching our kids running through the
yard. When we look at the world that way, any place and any
time can be sacred. It all depends on how we look at it. Who
is to say a tender interaction at the checkout counter can't feel
sacred? And surely there are plenty of congregations that feel
about as intimate as a subway station.

The word "spiritual," then, is a pointer to something beyond language. It is a vulnerable connection. As theology and
gender studies scholar Mark Jordan puts it, the spiritual is a
place of "unpredictable encounter or illumination that cannot
be controlled."

INVITATION

This book isn't going to introduce you to anything wildly new.
You already read, eat, walk, talk, and rest. You won't need to

buy a whole new set of spiritual tools. That's the gift of these traditions! All I'm inviting you to do is reframe your established habits through a lens of multilayered, deeper connection. Give intention to the evening cup of tea. Find community to discuss books that move and inspire you. Recite a little poem in the shower every morning. Whatever the practice is, we'll start by embracing it as something real and important, and we'll dive deeper to make it meaningful.

Because we're all different, some practices will come more easily to you than others. I connect most with the sacredness of life when I'm engaging with other people, for example. I love to sing, to play board games, and to eat with others. My husband, Sean, in contrast, will look at my weekly calendar and break out in hives because of the number of calls, meetings, and meals I've scheduled. His way of connecting is by being in the natural world or spending quality time on his own. On the other hand, I struggle to make time to be outside. One of the first moments when I knew that I loved him was when we went to the symphony together and halfway through the piece I turned to look at him and saw tears streaming down his face—not because he was upset, but because he was able to open himself to the beauty of the music and feel its depth and intensity resonating with his own life. How I wish for that kind of authenticity and vulnerability! Each of us has our own gifts, our own walkways through life and its mysteries, so be gentle with yourself as you discover what captures your attention and opens your heart.

This book is an invitation to explore the layers of experience that we can dive into in every practice. And as we do, struggling here and there, remember, there is nothing that can get between you and life's deepest connection. Nothing, no matter how powerful, can ever take that away. Not depression or anxiety, not assault or addiction, not grief or jealousy, not poverty or wealth. Each of us is entirely worthy and beloved. Even you. Especially you. Our shared human condition means that we forget this all the time, which is exactly why we practice. To help us remember.

So don't worry if you struggle here and there. Or with all of it. I've found that having friends and mentors with whom you can talk about this kind of stuff without feeling self-conscious suddenly makes it all much more doable. But whether you're an old hat or a spiritual beginner, whether you're a Potterhead or watching a nineties rom-com, you have everything that you need to take your next best step. Let's begin.

CHAPTER I

Connecting with Self

T HE FIRST LAYER of connection is the experience of being authentically connected to ourselves.

Surrounded as we are by hundreds of advertising messages a day and the pressures of social media, we move through the world with our bodies shamed and our attention drained. We can barely go to the bathroom or stop at a traffic light without checking our phones. I even struggle to take a shower without having a podcast playing in the background!

Writer Annie Dillard teaches us that how we spend our days is how we spend our lives. And this way of life is unsustainable. It is making us unwell. At least one in six American adults are on antidepressants, antianxiety medications, or antipsychotics, as reported by a study in *JAMA Internal Medicine* in 2016. Surely this says at least as much about our culture of incessant activity and pressure as it does about any of our individual medical needs.

So when do we reclaim our time and well-being? How can we give ourselves the space to reflect—deeply and honestly—about how we're doing? In this chapter I'll share with you two transformative practices for connecting with ourselves: sacred reading and sabbath time. Both these practices are gifts from our ancestors that allow us to bring intentional rituals to our modern lives. Like CrossFit and other secular practices that fulfill gaps in our hunger for meaning and community as we turn away from religion, sacred reading and sabbath time are things you probably already do that give you joy, a sense of purpose, a meditative space, and a feeling of connection to your authentic self. What's critical is that we see these daily rituals as part of a larger shift toward a new definition of spirituality.

Of course, the idea of a single, authentic self is worth considering. Indeed, Buddhist philosophy would tell us that there's no self at all. Psychology, on the other hand, says there are many selves to come home to! What I mean by connecting with our authentic self is less about stripping away the parts of ourselves that we don't like or focusing only on the bits that seem more spiritual, and more about integrating the fullness of who we are. Quaker activist and teacher Parker Palmer calls it rejoining our soul and our role because in the splitting of the two, much of our lost awareness and subsequent suffering appears.

I learned this the hard way. At age twenty-two, three months after graduating from university and starting my first job in London, I fell from a pier and broke both my lower legs and a wrist and double-fractured my spine. I spent weeks in the hospital and three months in a wheelchair, totally robbed of my busy activist life and young-professional persona. (I liked to imagine myself as Anne Hathaway's character, the second executive assistant, about two-thirds of the way through *The Devil Wears Prada*, as she aces tasks and looks fabulous doing it.) After the fall, however, instead of juggling meetings, calls, and emails, the major event of my day became a trip to the shower, carried up the stairs by my father and sister. Later, once I was a little more mobile in my wheelchair, I was constantly forced to recognize that the built environment was designed for walking people. Any small step or sidewalk bump caused serious challenges to my inexpert mobility skills in the chair. Whereas usually I took charge of social situations, I was now reliant on the care of others.

These role crises often appear at the end of a high-flying career when retirement strips us of our positional power and influence, or when our children leave home and we no longer occupy the easily recognizable role of parent, or when our health or physical abilities change. Who are we without the role that has given us meaning?

When we're lucky, these transitions can help us reconnect with our interiority, the awareness that lives behind the ego. Writer Marilynne Robinson phrases it like this: "The classic soul is more ourselves than we are, a loving and well-loved companion, loyal to us uniquely, entrusted to us, to whom we entrust ourselves. We feel its yearnings, its musings, as a truer and more primary experience of ourselves than our ordinary consciousness can offer us." I love that notion of total loyalty because it captures the inherent goodness of our authentic self, the compassion and friendship that live inside our deepest selves. But when we live disconnected from this inherent knowing, we get caught in cycles of performance and achievement, trying to please others' expectations or our perception of what is wanted of us.

The wisdom of tradition teaches us that there are ways out of this mess, that we can practice self-awareness and befriend our own souls gently and fiercely.

In my months of recovery after the fall, my mother invited a friend of hers to stop by on Wednesday mornings and paint with me. Unlike my sisters, I am no artistic talent, so I was hesitant because nothing frustrates me more than failing in public! I'm supposed to be good at things, my brain tells me, so why would I humiliate myself by trying to paint? During the long, quiet days of bed rest, I had watched endless episodes of *Strictly Come Dancing*, the British equivalent of *So You Think You Can Dance*, and so my painting teacher invited me to paint the steps that the dancers practiced each week. I tried to capture the waltz, the paso doble, and the rumba, letting the brushstrokes manifest the frustrations of a slow recovery, alongside the hope of being able to walk and dance again. Without really being conscious of it, this practice was a sanctuary. Like holy spaces in which the injured and sick once sought comfort, my kitchen table became a place for healing when I picked up a paintbrush, a place where I could process and detangle the heavy cocktail of emotions my accident had left me with. Sometimes we need the temporary isolation of enforced unplugging to bring into our awareness parts of ourselves that have been lying low. The great Japanese Zen teacher Kōdō Sawaki described his meditation practice as "the self selfing the self." The idea is that we need time and attention to integrate our experiences, ideas, and identities to be who we are.

This experience of seeing how a supposedly secular practice like painting could become a powerful, perhaps even spiritual, way of connecting to myself made me realize there were other small, seemingly insignificant rituals and habits that did the same thing. Years after I'd recovered from this fall at Harvard Divinity School and was knee-deep in our research for *How We Gather*, we found many such practices among the people we interviewed, including running and meditating. Yet there were two that stood out to us as the most accessible and most impactful for most of the people we'd studied: reading texts as sacred and resting in sabbath time.

Harry Potter as a Sacred Text

Mr. and Mrs. Dursley, of number four, Privet Drive, were proud to say that they were perfectly normal, thank you very much.

So begins the first book in J. K. Rowling's Harry Potter series. It's a sentence that millions of readers can quote off by heart, setting the scene as it does with a little humor and suggesting that something very *ab*normal is about to happen.

I read the Potter books enthusiastically as a teenager. I was thirteen when I was introduced to the series by my Parisian exchange student, who gave me a boxed set in French. After trying a few pages, I realized I'd be better off reading in English and headed to the library. I read the books and fell in love.

Perhaps you've had a similar experience with a book you adored: that sense of falling into its world, knowing the characters and landscapes intimately—even if they are invented in your mind. I usually know if this has happened when I read at the dinner table, so that the pages are stained with food or the corners are marked by my greasy fingers. More importantly, I trust you'll know that feeling of slowing down as the remaining chapters dwindle, not wanting the book to end. And then when our eyes scan those closing paragraphs, feeling that wave of loss and longing that go far beyond saying goodbye to the story we've read; it's more like saying goodbye to a piece of ourselves.

That sensation tells us something important. It suggests that reading is not just something we can do to escape the world, but rather that it can help us live more deeply *in* it, that we can read our favorite books not just as novels, but as instructive and inspirational texts that can teach us about ourselves and how we live.

We can treat a book as sacred not because we're going to

believe that the storylines within it somehow explain the mysteries of the universe, but because they help us be kinder, more compassionate. They help us be curious and empathetic. And they offer us a mirror in which we get to reflect on the motivations that live behind the actions we take every day. This is the power of reading books as a sacred practice: they can help us know who we are and decide who we might want to become.

Harry Potter holds a special place for me as a sacred text (more on that in a minute), but you can choose any piece of literature, poetry, or even nonfiction. What we'll explore in this chapter is the methodology of *how* to read as a sacred text. This will offer you countless new perspectives, insights about yourself, and opportunities to reflect on life questions. It may be a little unfamiliar, but trust me. Sacred reading has deepened my awareness and cultivated connection for readers for thousands of years.

THE ART OF SACRED READING

When we think about sacred texts, we think of the Bible, the Qur'an, the Torah, the Book of Mormon, or the Bhagavad Gita. We know these texts are full of stories, poems, and commandments. Some of the stories resonate, but much of traditional religious literature makes us suspicious. Their doctrine has been used to marginalize and malign. Saint Paul told women to stay silent in church. The Hebrew Bible condones slavery. The Qur'an demands punishment for same-sex love. But this is only part of the story. In spite of all the problems inherent in scriptures, they're continually studied and read because people believe that rereading these works might make us more faithful, more just, more loving; that the thousands of years in which generations have engaged these texts is something we need to pay attention to; and that we can step into a continuous stream of conversation between the text and human beings that has lasted centuries. In his book *To Know as We Are Known*, Parker Palmer explains why he keeps returning to sacred texts, despite their problems connected to a spiritual tradition in which people have sought and found wisdom through generations: "These texts allow me to return to times of deeper spiritual insights than my own, to recollect truths that my culture obscures, to have companions on the spiritual journey who, though long dead, may be more alive spiritually than many who are with me now. In such study my heart and mind are reformed by the steady press of tradition against the distortions of my day."

What I love about this insight is that traditional sacred texts can be bastions that push back against contemporary assumptions about who we are and what matters. Whenever I hear someone quote scriptural teachings against my gay love, it hurts. I can't deny that. But it also reminds me that what we deem right and wrong can change. It is entirely possible that, one day, we won't judge one another by how much we earn or what job title we have. And hearing stories of easy hospitality in Bible stories, for example, also teaches us that history is far from one-way progress. Palmer points us to the value of sacred texts because they are conversation partners that expand our reference points and force us to reflect on the culture we live in.

But what about those of us who don't fit into a religious box? Or don't know where to start with a text like the Bible? Or don't even want to trust a book like that? If this applies to you, my hope is that you'll join me in choosing a text of your own to treat as sacred—something you already love, that you already find yourself turning to again and again. We can all benefit from the ancient practices of sacred reading. We can find companions on our life's journey and draw on the wisdom of those who have come before us. Just imagine these textual ancestors walking along a path and sowing seeds, and now we are able to delight in the resulting flowers. And who knows, perhaps by engaging in these sacred practices in our own ways today we'll be planting seeds for others to enjoy when they travel this road in years to come.

So what defines a text as sacred in the first place? Traditionally, religious leaders have been the ones to decide what does and doesn't count. This is part of why some fundamentalists believe in the inerrancy of their texts—that they proclaim the absolute truth, and all evidence of dinosaurs be damned. Many Christians understand the life of Jesus to be the embodied word of God so that his actions as well as his words manifest as a sacred text. In my experience, many religious people understand a sacred text to be one in which the

words were somehow divinely inspired—there wasn't necessarily a godly author, but the words being put on the page were
channeled in some way or were written with a higher state of
consciousness.

Yet I offer a bold rebuttal: none of these definitions is
what makes a text sacred. It isn't about the author or the inspiration. As my mentor, Harvard Divinity School professor
Stephanie Paulsell, explains, a text is sacred *when a community says that the text is sacred.* It's that simple. When a group of
people returns year in, year out, to the same text, wrestling
with it by investing their questions, struggles, and joys—that's
what does it. It becomes generative, creating new responses
in text, music, movement, film, and story. When we understand a text to be sacred because a community says so, we
are given permission to infuse spiritual meaning into whatever text speaks to us.

Here's why this matters: it helps us reframe how we think
about the things that are sacred, holy, and important to us.
In everyday language, we think of "sacred" as an adjective,
as a synonym for "holy" or "blessed." It describes something
static, maybe a little dusty, outside our day-to-day experience.
But it is much better understood as a verb—something that
we *do.* The word "sacred" itself comes from the Latin *sacrare*,
which means to consecrate or dedicate. And to consecrate
means to declare or *make* something holy. So the sacredness
is in the doing, and that means we have enormous agency to
make "sacred" happen ourselves.

If this seems far-fetched, it's because we live under

the lasting influence of the great French sociologist Émile Durkheim, who made the distinction between the sacred and the profane. The name may or may not ring a bell, but the collective belief will sound familiar: that there are some things that count as religious, and others as secular. But let me ask you, is that reflective of your experience? I know that some of the most tender, intimate, perhaps even holy moments of my life have had nothing to do with formal religion: when I first held my niece in my arms, when I walked through a forest at age eleven, when I woke up from major surgery (mind you, that might have been the morphine). Our lived experience is a testament to the fact that transcendence and the deepest meaning we experience often come in the most "secular" moments, in that they have nothing to do with formal religion. (Ironically, religion at its best teaches us the same thing—but we'll come to that later.)

But celebrating our ability to claim something as sacred doesn't mean that every book we love reading immediately becomes a sacred text. It takes more than that.

CREATING *HARRY POTTER* AND *THE SACRED TEXT*

I first met Vanessa Zoltan at Harvard Divinity School. Like me, she was an unlikely divinity school candidate; she grew up Jewish but fiercely atheist. After all, she was raised with the notion that God died in Auschwitz. As all four of her grand-

parents were Holocaust survivors, the point was easily understood.

Vanessa intrigued me. On my birthday, a few days after
we met, she sent me an email with the subject line: "HAPPY
BIRTHDAY BRAND NEW FRIEND!" She was a keeper. We started
going for coffee, and one day she invited me to come to a
group she ran on Tuesday nights, reading *Jane Eyre* as a sacred
text. I had absolutely no idea what that meant, but I trusted
my instincts and agreed to join. I picked up a copy of Charlotte Brontë's classic from the library, read the prescribed
chapter, and headed into the New England fall evening to
meet her.

What happened was both bewildering and inspiring. With
a group of four other women, we sat around for an hour and a
half talking about a single chapter. It wasn't a book club conversation about what we thought about the plot, or why such-
and-such happened when Mr. Rochester had said so-and-so in
the chapter before. No, we were asking questions like, What
can we learn about suffering? How can we better understand
mental illness? What does the text ask us to do in our own
lives? I couldn't stop thinking about it.

The winter break was coming up. Boston winters are cold
and dark and a little depressing, so I wanted to find something that would help me beat the post-Christmas blues,
something that would feel like a grand adventure but still
allow me to eat snacks on the sofa. Vanessa and I had both
taken a class about epic journeys and quests, and her sacred
reading group had inspired me. Perhaps, I thought, we could

make our own meaning-making journey through a movie series. And if so, what better series than the magical Harry Potter films?

So for each day of the first week of January, Vanessa and I gathered a group of friends to re-watch the movies as if they were one enormous epic story—and we had an idea. What if we sat down to talk with other people, like her *Jane Eyre* group, and read Harry Potter as a sacred text?

And so we did. We promised one another we'd sit and read the books chapter by chapter, asking them what they might teach us about how to live. We'd use spiritual practices from antiquity, like PaRDeS and Florilegia, to dig underneath the plot to find unexpected wisdom in the wizarding world. I asked my sister to design a poster, and Vanessa asked her workplace if we could use their meeting space. We sent emails and invited friends, but we had no idea if anyone would come. On the first night, we put out twenty chairs, hoping we might have some curious visitors. Sixty-seven people came. We were thrilled!

As the group settled and we built a mini congregation where people made friends, visited one another in the hospital, and fell in love, we wondered if others might want to join our adventure. We launched *Harry Potter and the Sacred Text* as a podcast in May 2016, the same month I got married. We weaseled our way into the university's recording studio by bringing baked goods and chocolates to the administrative staff, and sat down behind the microphones. Neither of us had a broadcasting background, so it was largely thanks to our fellow Divinity School student Ariana Nedelman's production skills that we sounded at all cogent. Even today, at least a third of what we say in the studio gets left on the cutting-room floor.

The structure of the show is simple. Each week, we read a chapter through a theme in preparation for our conversation. For example, we started the series by reading Chapter One, "The Boy Who Lived," through the theme of commitment. Other themes have included forgiveness, trauma, delight, and love. In every episode we share a story from our own lives that relates to the theme, bring our listening community up to speed with a short recap of what happens in the chapter, and then enter into an ancient spiritual practice that helps us dig deeper into the text, and this is where the magic really happens.

Thanks to our incredible listeners, today *Harry Potter and the Sacred Text* is an award-winning podcast with over twenty-two million downloads and seventy thousand regular weekly listeners. Each year we go on tour and meet thousands of listeners who tell us what the practice of sacred reading has meant to them. People turn to the books and podcast for comfort in moments of crippling anxiety or loneliness. Sacred reading has helped people cope after the death of a loved one or a painful breakup. Teachers adapt the practices for classrooms to help students reflect more meaningfully on standard teaching texts. Over and over again we learn that these practices help people connect with what matters most to them.

Perhaps we shouldn't have been surprised that the podcast would become a success. Millions of readers already treated the Potter books as sacred in their own way. Therapists and counselors report young people using Hogwarts as their psychological safe place to go to in times of struggle and pain. And it isn't simply a refuge from the world. The Harry Potter Alliance, founded in 2005, has mobilized thousands around the country to act on marriage equality, fair-trade chocolate, and other progressive issues, using the narratives and rituals from the books to motivate and shape winning campaigns. Just as social justice movements have reinterpreted biblical narratives like the Exodus story and quoted the psalms, so too the Harry Potter Alliance references characters and plot lines from the wizarding world to motivate readers into action.

SACRED READING BRINGS US HOME TO OURSELVES

Reading Harry Potter with this lens has been transformative for me and the thousands of people who listen to *Harry Potter and the Sacred Text* because it helps us connect with our full selves. Reading makes us see ourselves in other characters, become nostalgic for parts of our past, and challenge our worldview. It's also often credited with helping people create empathy. Keith Oatley, a cognitive psychologist at the University of Toronto, made headlines in 2006 with his study that suggested reading about other people improves our ability to understand and cooperate with others and ultimately to understand ourselves. Many other studies have put forth similar arguments. But empathy doesn't start with others. It starts with yourself. In a German study from 2017, participants were taught to recognize different sub-personalities, such as our "happy voice" or "inner critic." By learning to engage critically our own various thought patterns, we become better able to infer the mental states of others. We become more empathetic.

Self-discovery through reading is often revelatory and freeing. But it isn't always pleasant. It makes us look within, and that is sometimes painful. We can be confronted by trauma and suffering when reading about someone who went through a similar experience, and we can be forced to address things we haven't before. Vanessa and I have become accustomed to receiving emails from listeners who reveal that the deep reading we've done on air brought up unresolved trauma like surviving sexual assault, for example. At the very start of the books, we learn that Harry's parents were killed in a horrific double murder that he, as a baby, somehow survived. Our sacred reading spoke to one listener in particular, who shared her story of a traumatic moment that shaped her life. When she was an infant, her father was killed in a terrorist attack in Latin America. She wrote:

> It's weird growing up knowing what evil has done to you, and what a stranger's hatred has caused you. It's weird growing up missing someone you've never met. Harry's undying love for Lily and James reassured me that it was okay for me to miss my dad, even though I had never met him. It was

okay for me to mourn the loss even though I hadn't been aware of it when it first happened. It is okay for me to still struggle with it and with some PTSD even though it's been 22 years and I never met him.

I feel a weird connection to Harry due to the nature of our losses, and your invitation to take that connection seriously has been so healing and soothing for me. It's also led me to see Harry's grief with very different eyes. It must be so difficult for him to navigate this world in which so many people he's never met know so much about his parents and remember them so clearly, and he just has to take their word for it. When I found out some stuff my dad had said and done that goes totally against what I believe in, I thought of Harry watching James bully Snape. It was so comforting knowing that James Potter wasn't perfect when it came to admitting to myself that my dad wasn't either. It deepened my connection to this story and this character, and I am so grateful I had that anchor when everything else I thought I knew was falling apart.

This letter illustrates that so much of what coming home to ourselves involves is the reminder that we are fundamentally okay, that our experience is valid even when we can't make total sense of it. And that sacred reading can help us find solid ground when the world around us is forever shifting.

There are times, conversely, when listeners tell us that sacred reading has helped them become something different, that by deeply reflecting on who they are, they have found something they want to transform. Take a look at this note from a listener who spent many years as a military commander in the armed forces, serving overseas. He refers to a scene where Ginny Weasley reminds Harry that she's previously been possessed by Voldemort and that his forgetting of this fact shows him just how lucky he is:

I thought I got where I was due to my own hard work, ambition and courage but as I reflect on it I realized I'm actually fairly lazy and cowardly. Once I started to actually see other people and see myself I realized that being an upper middle-class white man raised in a stable home had gained me more than my effort, ambition or courage. My classmate who worked her way to Cadet Wing Commander in college and into an F-15C Eagle fighter cockpit had given a lot more of that than me. My flight commander who graduated from Howard University, became an officer and raised two small kids while his wife finished her PhD had given a lot more of that than me. The young Airman from the backwoods of Tennessee who learned computer programing and enlisted in the Air Force to change his future had given a lot more of that than me. I started to realize that I've been blind. That's when your episode struck me.

. . . I finally decided that I needed to write you when I heard one line: "Lucky you." I'd read that line years ago barely noticing it and in no way considered the broader meaning Vanessa tied to it. I'd said many times that I didn't see color, and I believed it. Someone very close to me pointed out many

times that if I didn't see someone from an oppressed or un-
derprivileged group in light of what they had to deal with to
get to where they are, then I didn't really see them at all. . . .
For 40 years I thought I pulled myself up by my boot straps,
that I was more deserving of what I had than others and that
anyone who didn't reach what I defined as success failed due
to their shortcomings. I was wrong. . . . My privilege meant I
didn't have to think about anyone else. Lucky me.

Reading is a path to greater awareness. To courage and
commitment. To helping us see our mistakes, and to finding a
better way forward.

One very fateful reading of the early books that led to an
especially robust conversation among our listeners was about
Mrs. Petunia Dursley, who, believe me, is universally disliked.
As Vanessa and I reread that first chapter, we saw a young
woman, unsupported in motherhood, suddenly given a second infant to care for after the death of her sister. Imposed
on by a world she has always envied and feared, with no ex-
planation, she feels vulnerable to a society that can only spell
danger. No doubt, Petunia is abusive to Harry; she neglects
him in the most foundational years of his life. But this sacred
reading illustrated that narratives of good and evil nearly always are more complex when we risk our hearts to explore
a sacred reading. It not only gave me a new lens for understanding a character, but it challenged me to realize I'd let the
polarizing news narratives construct simplistic binaries of in-
nocence and guilt. I had long judged Mrs. Dursley, yet there

was a lot behind that judgment to be unpacked. This is why sacred reading can be a part of a spiritual practice of connecting to ourselves: it challenges us to look within. Sacred reading won't always make you popular. But it will help you get closer to the truth.

DEEPENING A PRACTICE TO CONNECT TO OURSELVES: *LECTIO DIVINA*

Reading can help us integrate different pieces of our experience into our full selves. How we read, then, matters in this process. We can read for amusement and escapism, which is all well and good (sometimes necessary), but we can also go deeper. Unbundling religious rituals can, once again, be a helpful tool for infusing meaning into our everyday practices. *Lectio divina*, literally meaning sacred reading, is one such ritual.

In the twelfth century, Guigo II wrote a little book—it's more of a pamphlet really—explaining exactly how to do it. He called the book *Scala Claustralium*, which translates from the Latin into *The Ladder of Monks*. In it, he describes how to read a text in four steps moving up a ladder, climbing ever closer to heaven. Those who are "God's lovers" may climb ever higher into the clouds and find themselves among a host of "heavenly secrets," he explains. He imagines angels carrying up fervent wishes and coming back down to reignite our desire for goodness.

Rather than reading entire chapters in the Bible, Guigo instructed his students to choose just a sliver of text to chew on. "Do you know how much juice has come from one little grape, how great a fire has been kindled from a spark, how this small piece of metal has been stretched on the anvil of meditation?" he asks. In fact, one need not even finish reading a sentence! The text can shower sweetness on the soul, restoring the weary mind with just a snippet. A century earlier, Saint Anselm had advised his wealthy patron, Countess Matilda of Tuscany, that if she read a sacred text her goal was not to finish reading it, but instead to read only as much as would stir her mind to prayer. Medieval scholar Duncan Robertson explains that "the fulfillment of reading [began] in the moment the reader [lifted] her eyes from the page and [took] an active part in what [was] now a dialogue." Monastic communities didn't read a book only once—there were far too few precious volumes for that anyway! Rereading, and reading out loud, were how monks studied a text, leading them up the ladder. The text itself was a doorway into reflection and meditation. It was a sacred path to journey along into the heart of God. This might resonate for you if you find yourself rereading a favorite book. Or perhaps there are passages that evoke something for you, and you look up from the page just to drink in that sweetness or beauty.

In his pamphlet, Guigo furthered centuries of sacred reading instruction and simplified his guidance into the four steps of a ladder. He named these as reading, meditating, praying, and contemplating. The way Vanessa and I have translated this on the *Harry Potter and the Sacred Text* podcast is to think of these four stages as four sets of questions.

1. What's literally happening in the narrative? Where are we in the story?
2. What allegorical images, stories, songs, or metaphors show up for you?
3. What experiences have you had in your own life that come to mind?
4. What action are you being called to take?

The difference between simply reading a text and engaging this kind of meaning-making was, for Guigo's contemporary William of Saint-Thierry, "the same gulf . . . as there is between friendship and acquaintance with a passing guest, between boon companionship and chance meeting." This is the difference between reading for mere amusement and reading for self-knowledge and wisdom.

If you're feeling skeptical, I don't blame you. But let me share my own sacred reading of the opening line of Harry Potter. Together, we can see how *lectio divina* can dig underneath the surface and help us create opportunities for self-discovery. Here's the sentence. (I recommend saying the sentence out loud as we go through these questions. It helps make the text new every time you come back to it.)

Mr. and Mrs. Dursley, of number four, Privet Drive, were proud to say that they were perfectly normal, thank you very much.

Stage 1: What's literally happening in the narrative? Where are we in the story?

Even someone who is entirely new to the wizarding world can participate here. We know nothing more than these opening lines! Clearly, we're meeting a couple—Mr. and Mrs. Dursley—and they live in a house at number four Privet Drive. They desperately want to be seen as ordinary, and there's a self-satisfied bluntness to them that immediately makes us wary.

This first step is usually the simplest to do, and it's the level at which most of our everyday reading takes place. Do I know what's going on? Great, time to move on to the next sentence. But this is only the beginning of our sacred reading journey, the lowest rung on Guigo's ladder. Now we dig a little deeper. Read the sentence out loud again, and ask yourself—

Stage 2: What allegorical images, stories, songs, or metaphors show up for you?

Mr. and Mrs. Dursley, of number four, Privet Drive, were proud to say that they were perfectly normal, thank you very much.

A host of things immediately strike me. The word "Privet" sounds like "private"—so there's an element of hiding from the public eye. A privet is also a type of shrub, often used in hedges, suggesting another barrier between the Dursleys and us, the reader. But then it also reminds me of *privet*, the Russian word for "hi," so perhaps there's some willingness to cross the boundaries for guests from Moscow?! (Things don't always make sense on the second rung of the ladder.)

The number four is worth exploring too. There are four sides to a square, and the Dursleys are clearly a square kind of people. The most common meter in written music is the 4/4 beat, again suggesting normalcy. As a Divinity School graduate, I can't help but associate four with Buddhism's core teaching of the Four Noble Truths. So I am reminded of the inescapability of suffering and that the path to enlightenment is through nonattachment. Similarly, I think of the Four Horsemen of the Apocalypse, the four gospels, the four seasons, the four suits of a deck of cards. The Beatles. Four calling birds. The way in which people replace the letter "A" with a numeral "4" in computer passwords. The list is endless.

As you can see, in this second stage the only limit is your imagination. You could say that the words "thank you very much" remind you of Elvis. Or that "proud" sounds like "shroud" and that this might be a hidden metaphor for impending death, especially when combined with pride coming before a fall.

Guigo would tell us that the first stage is as if we're putting a bite of food into our mouths, and that in this second stage we have been chewing it, breaking it down into many smaller pieces. Our minds have been opened, and we're suddenly engaging images and words far beyond the boundaries of the text. We're connecting unexpected dots and layering in new associations. But at this stage we're delighting in a bundle of ideas—next we need it to resonate more deeply, to seek the spiritual meaning. In the third question, we connect the text explicitly to our own lives. As Guigo would say, we start to taste the flavor of the passage we've chosen, by asking—

Stage 3: What experiences have you had in your own life that come to mind?

Mr. and Mrs. Dursley, of number four, Privet Drive, were proud to say that they were perfectly normal, thank you very much.

The first thing that strikes me reading it this time is that Mrs. and Mr. Dursley are a married couple. My husband, Sean, and I have been married for a couple of years, and like most couples I know, we have some silly secret names for one another. The Dursleys, too, must have these nicknames. Despite their frustrations with one another, they are a team. They are raising their infant son, doing the best they can in a world that hasn't always been kind to them.

And I'm wondering who in the sentence is doing the saying, here? Does that individual speak on behalf of the couple, or is one voice taking the upper hand without consent? I know sometimes I'll write a card on behalf of my husband and myself to someone Sean barely knows. Or I will confidently buy tickets to go see a band that he perhaps isn't a huge fan of. So is it just Mrs. or Mr. Dursley who is proud of being normal? Perhaps there's more of a difference between the two than we originally assumed. It wouldn't be the first time a couple finds some unexpected differences after they tie the knot.

See how we're already learning more about the characters and facing some less-than-glamorous truths about ourselves? By layering into the story our own experiences, we understand the context of the Dursleys in a much deeper way. But so far, we're still bringing our ideas and reflections *to* the text. We haven't finished our journey up the ladder just yet. Now, in the fourth stage, we invite the text to speak to *us*. Guigo would have framed this as asking God to respond to our prayer, but

Vanessa and I prefer to simply imagine what the text might have to say to us.

Fair warning: this can be uncomfortable. Sacred reading isn't always pleasant, as we've explored. It can bring up difficulty and pain, even if only because reading something as if it is sacred means that we have to be willing to be changed. If our hearts and our imagination and our commitment to our deepest values have not expanded through a sacred reading practice, then we haven't been reading sacredly. So, to our final stage of the ladder—

Stage 4: What action are you being called to take?

Mr. and Mrs. Dursley, of number four, Privet Drive, were proud to say that they were perfectly normal, thank you very much.

Sometimes what the text calls us to do is life changing. Maybe we let go of an ancient hurt. Or we step up to a new responsibility. One podcast listener told us that she had, after years of thinking about it, signed up to become an adoptive parent after reflecting on how Harry Potter is welcomed into the Weasleys' family home. Other times, what we're called to do is simple and fun. I'm writing this while away from my husband and I miss him enormously, so in this moment, I feel called to send him a text message with one of my nicknames for him, to let him know that I'm thinking of him and that I love him. The connection between the text itself and our inspired action doesn't need to be logical. Sometimes, the nudges from the text to help us live with more courage, love, and integrity are delightfully mysterious.

Applying this short reflective exercise to various things

I have read over the years has unearthed a multitude of thoughts and feelings that have helped me settle into a deeper knowing of myself. Often these insights aren't necessarily new, but I had lost track of them. The sacred reading practice brings them back home, like a cat that slipped out the door when I wasn't looking and now needs a hand to come back inside. In this particular reading, I've been reminded of my inherent selfish streak. I get caught up in the work I am doing, which makes me feel good about myself and lose sight of the person who is most important to me. I have to remember that relationships of meaning need time and attention.

Of course, Guigo is only one teacher of sacred reading. On the podcast, we've learned from Saint Ignatius's teaching of sacred imagination—the practice of placing ourselves into the story we read as a character in the text—in order to better engage with the reading. Saint Ignatius's concept of sacred imagination also invites us to notice all our senses—what we hear, see, touch, smell, and taste. This encouragement to immerse ourselves in a story allows us to look beyond the words of the page to see what the characters are wearing and what they're doing when they're not speaking. It's as if a familiar image goes from black and white into full color, with new subtleties emerging about the world on the page, and the world in which we live. By finding more empathy for the characters on the page, we find more empathy for the people we share our lives with.

Of course, Christians aren't the only ones with sacred reading practices: Jewish communities have long engaged in havruta, a traditional rabbinic approach to Talmudic study in which a pair of students analyzes and discusses a shared text. Often, this is done by asking one another a question gleaned from the pages of the text. For example, in Harry Potter, why do owls appear at times of transition in the story? In this practice, it isn't enough to just ask a question of your learning partner—you must also propose a potential answer. Could it be that owls are able to turn their heads all the way around and that therefore moments of change are inevitably moments where we are forced to consider every aspect of our lives? How might we then notice these birds in the text? Having a consistent havruta study partner means not only that you are always challenged with new and exciting questions, but also that you build a bank of references together and that the truth to each wondering lies somewhere between you, always living in the back-and-forth of your questions and suggested answers. Together with your havruta partner and the text, you form a triangle in the middle of which the true insights of wisdom lie.

Lectio divina, Saint Ignatius's sacred imagination, and havruta have more than sacred reading in common; they all have the potential to be brought into secular spaces. Since introducing this idea on the podcast, Vanessa and I have heard many stories of how people are adapting these practices into their lives. Numerous teachers have started to adapt *lectio divina* for the classroom, creating four-part homework assignments or conversation prompts for their students. Others led sacred imagination with core curriculum texts. We've heard from families who listen to the show on long car journeys and then have havruta-style conversations to pass the time together. Perhaps most striking was at our first live show at a dingy bar in Cambridge, Massachusetts, when we had 375 people devouring a snippet of text in *lectio divina* while the beer was flowing all around us. I hope Guigo would have approved.

Beyond the Page:
Sacred Reading in the World

Reading is inherently about more than mechanistically decoding symbols on a page. It's about interpreting characters and the situations they find themselves in. It's about making meaning of the world around us. Reading changes us. We discover who we might become by the things we read—expanding our imagination with every new book we encounter.

Of course, there are other similar practices that bring us home to ourselves, and it's different for everyone. Long-distance speed-skating, chanting, double Dutch, ballroom dance, rock collecting, going for walks with your dog—what works for you might be ridiculed or seem insignificant to others. But take heart! Have conviction in your practice, no matter what others or your insecurity may tell you. There will be days when your practice feels empty. Pointless, even. Vanessa explains that in these moments we have to trust our former selves, who in times of clarity and conviction decided that this practice was the right thing to do. Like a student deciding to cheat at three in the morning, hours before the deadline, we can make our worst decisions when we're in distress. Conviction will help us make it through these trying moments to return once again to our sacred practices of connection. We have to have faith in the practice itself, even when we feel lost or like it isn't "working." So explore whether reading might be a practice that speaks to you and brings you a sense of connecting with your deeper self.

To be clear, finding a text to treat as sacred shouldn't limit you to Harry Potter. You might choose a literary classic, an obscure childhood favorite, or a poem. If you grew up bilingual, I highly recommend choosing a text in the language you were raised with. Often these words have an added resonance that can be heart opening. In fact, you can go beyond the printed word completely. You might choose the text of a song you grew up with, for example, or you can even choose a picture. Dutch theologian Henri Nouwen wrote an entire book focused on the sacred reading of a single Rembrandt painting. He shares the story of sitting in front of the image in the Hermitage Museum in Saint Petersburg. With every passing hour he unearths another layer of meaning, finding himself in all three of the characters depicted on the canvas. Or the text you choose can be performed, with an audience specifically invited to reflect on what the text means in their lives.

Stories were a big part of my childhood, and not just the bedtime variety. I realize looking back that hearing and reading stories were incredibly influential on my sense of self. Every twenty-third of December, my mother hosted a fundraiser and invited our famed village storyteller to perform at our house. The living room would be transformed—every chair we owned was brought in, pillows were piled on the floor, and suddenly it seated forty-five people with a tiny little stage area by the door.

This, I learned as I got older, is not normal. It turns out not every village has its own storyteller. But Forest Row is the sort of place where it wasn't out of the question to see a classmate's mother taking her goat for a walk, so a storytelling school fit right in.

Every year, I'd look forward to Ashley Ramsden's rendition of Charles Dickens's *A Christmas Carol*. This is where I first learned that stories can be a mirror in which we reflect on our lives. Through character and plot, we start to understand more about who we are and how we live. And if we return again and again to the same story (as I did each year of my childhood), we will find new depths and new truths—about the text, but also about the world and our place in it.

You might have watched the Muppets' version or read the original classic, but the story is the same. Ebenezer Scrooge hates Christmas and sits in his office focused only on money, mistreating his clerk, Bob Cratchit, and everyone else he meets during the day. One Christmas Eve, Scrooge returns from his icy office and makes himself a bowl of gruel. He's already had the startling experience of seeing his deceased business partner Jacob Marley's face in his front door knocker. "It's all humbug" is as much as he can say to that. As Scrooge settles in for bed, he suddenly hears a strange clanging coming from downstairs. It's all the more unsettling because he has double-locked the door, and the noise is now coming up the stairs and moving ever closer.

Marley's ghost walks in. He enters Scrooge's bedroom, carrying an endless chain of heavy cash boxes, padlocks, and caskets of gold clasped to his ghoulish form. Marley bemoans his fate and tells Scrooge the same unhappy end awaits him if he does not change his ways. In a state of terror, Scrooge tries to reason with Marley, asking how he can be so tormented in the afterlife when he was always a good man of business? Marley replies in a full howl:

"BUSINESS!? HUMANITY WAS MY BUSINESS!"

I can hear Ashley the storyteller shouting this even now. It unsettles me still.

Now, it might seem that this performance was just a fun pastime. But that judgment would underestimate my mother, who organized this event every year. You see, my father too was a man of business. And so were plenty of other people in that living room. My dad was an investment banker, and his love for free-market economics didn't always leave oceans between him and Ebenezer Scrooge. This story has always carried special meaning for me because it reminds me that each one of our hearts hardens if we don't keep prying it open to the hurting world. It can be easier to check our bank balance than our conscience. So this story wasn't just entertainment. It was a call to action. Scrooge's own transformation was an invitation to everyone in that room to change our miserly ways, to embrace our common humanity, to redistribute wealth—not only for the sake of equality and justice, but also for the sake of our own liberation! We all sat down to engage this performed piece of text because we knew it would call us to a more loving view of the world.

At the beginning of the story, Scrooge refuses an invitation from his nephew Fred to come and play games on Christmas Eve. He has convinced himself that isolation and accumulating wealth are what make him happy. But the ghosts prove him wrong. And so, at the end of the story, he walks up to his nephew's house, where festive games are underway, and haltingly asks, "Will you let me in, Fred?" In that moment he's asking to be let into a house, to be readmitted into his own family, to be forgiven for his selfishness, and to rebuild his sense of identity not on how much he owns, but on how much he loves. Young as I was, I learned that a story could inspire and instruct us to live lives of meaning and purpose, connection and joy. But it didn't just happen by itself. It took someone—in this case, my mother—to set an intention, bring people together, bake a huge number of Christmas cookies, and repeat the event each year.

This is the wisdom of treating a text as sacred. It brings us closer to who we are, deep down. It helps us integrate our experiences. It helps us see beyond ourselves so that we can then turn back and see ourselves more clearly. To paraphrase thirteenth-century theologian and philosopher Thomas Aquinas, sacred texts teach us a truth vital for our lives that we couldn't discover by ourselves. They act as a mirror in which we confront attitudes and behaviors that we want to let go of. They can inspire us and ennoble who we want to become. Perhaps you've already chosen Harry Potter, or perhaps you prefer Toni Morrison. It might be Shakespeare or Isabel Allende. Or you might return to a traditional sacred text with a new way of reading. All of it is welcome. When we read sacredly, any of these—and so many more—can accompany us up the ladder toward an eternal sweetness that is always waiting for us.

Sabbath Time

Making time for ourselves is more and more difficult. Our digital devices distract us, offering us a life where everything is available at the recognition of a fingerprint, and being "busy" is likely the first thing we tell people when they ask how we are. This makes it difficult to even be aware of our inner life, or how we're really feeling. We can go for days without noticing that we're angry and resentful, for example, or that we've spent the last week particularly anxious, until that "difficult conversation" that we were anxious about has passed.

Shabbat, or sabbath, the ancient practice of rest in the Jewish tradition, offers us a model that we can draw on to create a modern ritual of making space for connecting to ourselves. Sabbath is about taking some much-needed soul time. When we make a conscious choice to enter a sabbath—creating a rule about when we do and won't do things, setting boundaries on screen time, whatever it may be—we create a pillar of clarity in our spiritual lives.

Sabbath has verified practical benefits too. A 2014 study looked at Seventh-day Adventists, a Christian group, who are known for strict sabbath observance and demonstrated a significant link between sabbath keeping and mental and physical health. A tight-knit community of nine thousand Adventists in Loma Linda, California, has been labeled as a "Blue Zone"—an area where people live much longer than the national average. Similarly, researchers have established that there are fewer adult deaths in Israel on Shabbat. So let's explore what sabbath can look like for those of us looking for deeper connection with ourselves.

Through our research of case studies for *How We Gather*, we found that in our modern lives, sabbath can be applied especially usefully in three ways: tech sabbath, sabbath for solo time, and sabbath for play and creativity. Of course, the traditional Jewish Shabbat is centered on shared celebration with others—and we'll explore more of that communal connection in the next chapter. But these sabbath practices are focused on helping us connect with our authentic selves.

Tech Sabbath

When I first arrived at Harvard Divinity School, I didn't think of myself as spiritual. I came because I wanted to learn about building community. I imagined myself having to sift through the curriculum to glean the useful bits while throwing out chunks of hocus-pocus that made no sense to me. Instead, I was surprised time and again by the broad and counterintuitive understanding of "religion" that my professors offered. And it wasn't just what happened in the classroom that expanded my imagination. It was normal for a meeting to start with a few moments of quiet meditation. On Wednesdays, the students, faculty, and staff gathered for a service led by a rotating series of student groups offering the riches of their traditions. This kind of learning environment allowed us all to be more human with one another. It turns out that academic discussions are much more fulfilling when you have a sense of someone's life story before you hear their perspective! All this is to say, I was a little skeptical about anything overtly religious being helpful to me as a modern, secular person, even after enrolling in divinity school.

One day, while perusing the library, I checked out Abraham Joshua Heschel's book *The Sabbath* on a whim. This short text floored me. I'd assumed that sabbath-keeping was an anachronistic hangover from shtetl life. Not turning on light switches and having to prepare all the food you'd want to eat a day before seemed irrelevant to my technology-powered lifestyle. But I realized that my tech use was getting in the way of actually enjoying myself. I'd long ago started the habit of waking up to my phone's alarm in the morning, making its glowing screen the first thing I looked at every day. I'd scroll through social media, check emails, and read the news before even getting out of bed. My focus was shattered, and any centered calm was long gone by the time I went to brush my teeth—all the while listening to a podcast. "Addiction" is a big word to use, but when I found myself checking my phone compulsively while cycling to school, it was clear that I had a problem. As artist Jenny Odell writes in her fabulous book *How to Do Nothing*, nothing is harder to do these days than doing nothing.

Heschel published his book in 1951, the year superglue was invented and the first commercial computer was sold. But already he knew how best we should engage modern technology. "The solution to mankind's most vexing problems will not be found in renouncing technical civilization, but in attaining some degree of independence from it," he wrote. He proposed that we find a way to live with new technologies and to do without them—not to abolish technology or turn back time, but to be intentional about how we use it. And to practice this, we have the sabbath. For one day a week, Heschel teaches us to live independently from our most important tools of production and to embrace the world—and ourselves—as we find it.

So, inspired by Heschel and a second text on sabbath by Wayne Muller, I made Friday nights a sacred time of digitally disconnecting from the outside world to make space for connecting with myself. Since 2014, I have been observing a "tech sabbath"—twenty-four hours of not using my laptop or phone from Friday sundown to Saturday sundown. No email, no social media, no nothing. As darkness comes, I stand in front of my window and watch the sky for a few moments. Then I light a candle, and while holding it, I sing a song I learned in childhood to enter the magical and mysterious sabbath time. The moment I put the candle back on the table I can feel it: my shoulders relax, my breath comes easier, and usually, the tiredness that I've been able to hold off catches up with me, and I'm in bed by nine o'clock. If I'm really feeling it, I'll light incense. Without my tech, there's no music or podcasts to listen to, so I'm in silence, often for the first time in days. I am suddenly given the opportunity (or forced, depending on the day) to look inward.

This practice of "resting" from technology is quite different from everyday life, where the world is ours to consume—to be selected, filtered, tapped, and enjoyed. Tech indelibly shapes our reality. We work, shop, unwind, and find love on our pocket-size screens. And as convenient as it is, we're undone by our compulsion to check the feeds, scrolling deep into the night. Technologist Kevin Kelly explains that it takes every new technology a decade before society comes to consensus on what etiquette we need to tame it. For example, it was ten years after the cell phone was invented that manufacturers introduced the option of a silent, or vibrate, mode. And because real conversations have difficulty competing with even a silent phone, we're in the midst of learning when to put phones out of sight or even, if we're brave, to turn them off altogether. Our mobile devices grant us three wishes, explains founding director of the MIT Initiative on Technology and Self Sherry Turkle in her book *Reclaiming Conversation*: "first, that we will always be heard; second, that we can put our attention wherever we want it to be; and third, that we will never have to be alone." That final wish denies us a crucial experience of connection—to our authentic selves.

Canadian researchers have demonstrated that staring into screens leaves us distracted, distant, and drained. A 2018 study from the University of British Columbia found that people who use phones during social interactions have less enjoyment of time spent with friends and family, while another study led by Sara Konrath at Indiana University concluded that those who struggle to identify and process their emotions use social media more often than those who are in touch with their feelings. This is worrying, as the average American now spends ten hours a day looking at a screen. We're even looking when there's nothing to see! Sixty-seven percent of cell phone owners check their phone for messages or other alerts even when they don't notice their phone vibrating or ringing. And it isn't just how we feel during the day. A 2016 University of Pittsburgh study concluded that young adults who spend a lot of time on social media are more likely to suffer sleep disturbance than their peers. All of which points to the value of taking a regular and total break from our tech.

Filmmaker Tiffany Shlain has long been a champion of tech sabbaths. In her online video series *The Future Starts Here*, she explains, "I love technology—but I feel like I'm constantly responding to everyone and not really responding to myself. A few years ago, I started thinking a lot about time. My father was dying of brain cancer, and sometimes he only had one good hour a day. So it made me think about how little time we have. During that time my family and I decided to completely unplug from technology for one day a week." Tiffany was inspired by the National Day of Unplugging—one day in the year where normal technology users are challenged to take a break and put their cell phone in a mini sleeping bag in which it can safely rest, while Unpluggers spend time gardening, talking with one another, or simply resting. Putting my tech out of sight has become essential. If I can see my laptop or phone lying around, it is amazing how tempting it can be to go onto social media or check my email. Especially when it gets to three on Saturday afternoon and I'm a little bored of reading!

During the week, Shlain describes herself as being in an "emotional pinball machine," barraged by emails, calls, and alerts. When her tech sabbath arrives, "it's like a valve of pressure releases from facts, articles and tidbits that I consume daily. I feel so much more grounded and balanced," she explains. "I feel like a better mother, wife, and person."

Surprisingly, I've learned that I don't need to be responsive all the time. Since putting a small note in my email signature that reads, "I am offline from sundown on Friday to sundown on Saturday, when I observe a tech sabbath," I'm often asked if I'm not worried about missing an urgent call. So far, no emergencies have struck and no once-in-a-lifetime opportunities have been lost. And even if I did miss an urgent call, that cumulative restful time might still be worth it.

Taking time away from our technology gives us the space,

time, and energy to reconnect to ourselves. We can slow down mentally and physically. I love to journal on my sabbath days, writing stream-of-consciousness thoughts and often finding new ideas or inspiration as my brain unwinds itself from the tight curl it's been wrapped up in. Heschel writes, "We must not forget that it is not a thing that lends significance to a moment; but it is the moment that lends significance to things." But unless we take the time away from incessant interruption, we cannot be present to that significance. With a tech sabbath, we can finally be present to ourselves and the significance of being alive.

SABBATH FROM OTHERS

We can bring sabbath into our modern lives to create connection with ourselves by taking a sabbath from others. For some people, this is their Sunday night bath. For others, it is a long run alone. Whatever it is, I invite you to make it intentional and set clear boundaries so you can make sure to honor your time alone.

My husband has learned that my sabbath time is more than a chance for me to get away from work emails and Twitter threads—it is also about being on my own. He generously spends a few hours out running errands or going to see a movie, giving me the ultimate luxury of some space and time all to myself. Although as a Harvard proctor I live with twenty-eight college freshmen down the hall, a weekly sabbath offers a mini staycation of sorts, a chance to mentally reset and spiritually re-center.

Sabbath isn't a time to catch up on tasks. Nor is it simply a time of rest to prepare for a busy week. It is a time to revel in the beauty and delight of simply being. The sabbath "is not for the purpose of recovering one's lost strength and becoming fit for the forthcoming labor," Heschel writes. "The sabbath is a day for the sake of life. . . . The sabbath is not for the sake of the weekdays; the weekdays are for the sake of sabbath." This was a revelation to me: to think of sabbath time as the apex of the week, a "climax of living." I started to look forward to the times when I'd read for the sake of pleasure, rather than learning or productivity. I read historical fiction like the novels of Maurice Druon and found myself in science fiction adventures with N. K. Jemisin. Reading during sabbath time opened up new worlds because I was free from the constraints I'd built myself. "The point about the novel is that you're free in your head," writes journalist Robert McCrum in an interview with Five Books. "It's unpoliced. Reading really does liberate you."

Sabbath inverts some of the most destructive stories we tell ourselves: that we are what we do, that we're worth only what we create. "The sabbath is the inspirer, the other days are the inspired," writes Heschel. We're allowed to be the fullness of who we are and have the space to dive deeply into difficult questions or decisions. We can take time to ponder things, to think thoughts through to the end without interruption. In silence and solitude, we rediscover childhood passions. Sabbath is all about remembering who we truly are.

That can feel strange at first. So much of our lives is spent hovering in the unfulfilling no-man's-land between true solitude and deep community. Parker Palmer argues that this is where the prevailing sense of vacuousness comes from, that our lives "alternate between collective busyness and individual isolation but rarely allow for an authentically solitary or corporate experience. In this half-lived middle ground, our solitude is loneliness and our attempts at community are fleeting and defeating." Sabbath from collective busyness not only frees us from distraction but gives us time alone so that we can dip down into our experience consciously, letting our minds wander. I've found myself pulling out paper and pastels or a songbook. Now and then I write a poem. With this luxury of sabbath time, we get to explore creative parts of ourselves that the everyday keeps hidden under lock and key. In the Age of the Screen, there is little room for amateur creativity. We feel no permission to sing or dance because we've seen what it *should* look like when professionals perform. We're never free to learn a craft because the horror of someone seeing our imperfect work is paralyzing. In sabbath time, our creativity is not meant for performance—but for enjoyment, and perhaps even as an offering of thanks for the time and freedom we have.

You probably do some or all of these things already. But it might take an intentional shift to start thinking of this time as a sacred time for solitude. I invite you to change that. Whatever your practice is, make it an intentional ritual. Light a candle. Recite a poem. Breathe ten times. Whatever you do, try to notice how taking this time heals and softens you. Our inner life is the foundation for our outer lives, so committing to this practice will yield countless gifts. This is the paradigm shift: everyday moments can be the sacred foundation of your spiritual life.

Sabbath from Work to Make Room for Play

Although sabbath time involves putting daily tools away, it is not about depriving ourselves. The opposite is true. What can we learn about ourselves when we press PAUSE on work and productivity and make space for playtime? Traditionally, the sabbath is a time for joy and fullness. Delicious food, good company—even sex is a mitzvah (Jewish religious duty) during sabbath time! So wonderful is Shabbat that Jews traditionally observe it for twenty-five hours instead of a full day—delighting in the time of rest so much that there's a desire to keep hold of it for one extra hour. Customarily, the sabbath is received as a queen or a bride—the home is cleaned, and each member of the household looks their best. Inspired by this tradition, I like to pretend that sabbath time is like going to a royal wedding. I'm lucky to be invited, and I'm going to make the most of enjoying it! If you're exploring a sabbath practice, I invite you to discover how you might create some rituals that help you cross into sabbath time and that can unleash your creative or playful spirit!

Sabbaths can be longer than just a day—and can of course

be celebrated with others. One of the case studies from our *How We Gather* research was Camp Grounded, a summer camp for adults. Set up in 2013, Camp Grounded describes itself like this: "Imagine a place where adults completely let go, get really, really weird, laugh uncontrollably, sing during meals, and stay up late sharing secrets until they fall asleep in a tipi . . . only to wake-up a few hours later to [enjoy] . . . sunrise paddle-boarding or morning yoga, endless arts 'n crafts and silly competitions. They dress in funny costumes, dance a lot, perform at the talent show, call each other nicknames and play super super hard. All without the use of drugs or alcohol, without being instagrammed or updating their status online, and without talking about what they do for work. It's surreal and amazing."

Set up by Levi Felix, Camp Grounded took the principles of sabbath time and created a weeklong experience based on those rules. Getting away from technology and workplace identities allowed campers to reconnect with their innate creativity. To paint and sing, to laugh and be silly. To write handwritten letters and sit around the campfire. Felix set up Camp Grounded after a serious health scare interrupted an eighty-hour-a-week work schedule and total focus on his career. It reminded him to work on what he really cared about. Tragically, after four years of Camp Grounded magic, he died of a brain tumor. But he has left a legacy. "He was a catalyst for so many people to get in touch with themselves and spark meaningful conversations," explains one friend, Andrew Horn.

Summer camp has always echoed sabbath time for me too. When I was eleven years old, I arrived at a rural Dutch train station to be met by camp leaders in funny costumes who cycled with us to the edge of the campground. There they started a conga line "spaceship" so we could travel through time together. All our watches were turned forward two hours (so campfires could be enjoyed earlier in the day), and only after we'd entered the "camp time zone" could we walk onto the field where our tents and the firepit stood waiting. No need for epic structures or distant journeys, we could step into a different reality through a small ritual and large amounts of enthusiasm. Though camp rules and mentality might not be possible all year round, it was at least waiting for us to return to its sweet playfulness and joy whenever we were ready. This is what Heschel meant when he called the sabbath a palace in time. Or imagine a beautiful cathedral in time. We enter it with the same awe and inspiration. Indeed, crossing into sabbath means crossing into an encounter with the divine reality, wherever we are. There's no need for a physical temple or a church, or even a beautiful forest. That is the beauty of sacred time: it stretches across all places and is accessible to us, wherever we are.

Here is the beauty of sabbath for exploring play: it's really sabbath for exploring you. If you were anything like me, you learned at summer camp that you weren't half bad at making crafts. Maybe through sabbath you will discover that you take great joy from playing an instrument, something you would have never carved out time to consider had you not established a set period of rest from everything else. Of course, learning a new skill or mastering something isn't the goal of sabbath. You don't have to, and in fact shouldn't, play for a purpose. Hobbies don't have to become hustles! Making room for play is about learning what things awaken joy for you, and making time for those special things.

BRINGING SABBATH INTO OUR LIVES

Remember what I promised you at the beginning of this book: you are already doing most of these practices. All we are preparing to do is simply the next step of deepening them and giving them intention. You probably already have some self-care fallbacks that help you find solitude, or a few tricks for finding "me time." Maybe you already try to limit screen time. Maybe you do yoga every Thursday to get away from your desk, the kids, or whatever it is that occupies most of your time. My invitation is to turn those practices into regular, sacred times of sabbath. Put it on the calendar. Make it a rule.

Though I've chosen to stick to the traditional timing, sabbath doesn't need to be restricted to Friday nights. We can enter sabbath time whenever we want—though tradition recommends a regular rhythm. By Wednesday I'm usually already fantasizing about my Friday night tech sabbath, which always involves a lengthy shower and special moisturizing routine to welcome in the mini retreat! Discipline is key—and is the thing I struggle most with, especially when I'm away from home. Heschel's advice would have been stern: "What we are depends on what the sabbath is to us." When we keep a sabbath, we get to practice saying "no." No one will enforce it for us. Our employers will always be grateful for the extra hours we work. We must be the ones to choose sabbath, and that is profoundly difficult! Stopping is often the last thing I want to do. I worry that stopping means failing at something because to stop makes no sense amid the rules of competition and the culture of progress. Tricia Hersey, the creator of the Nap Ministry, describes rest as a form of resistance, because it pushes back against capitalism and white supremacy. "Our bodies are a site of liberation," she explains on her website. Her work counters the narrative that we are all not doing enough and should be doing more. To stop work forces us to play by a different set of rules, just like Felix and his Camp Grounders did. Our inner perfectionist must die just a little every time, and the death can be painful, humiliating even. But the promise of rest, of new life, of a world transformed holds true every time. I often say to myself that the work is not done, and yet it is still time to stop.

Ultimately, a sabbath of some form or another is necessary for connecting with ourselves. The great writer and monk Thomas Merton wrote in his book *No Man Is an Island*, "We do not live more fully merely by doing more, seeing more, tasting more, and experiencing more than we ever have before. On the contrary, some of us need to discover that we will not begin to live more fully until we have the courage to do and see and taste and experience much less than usual." Merton urges us to find our real self, even if that simple dignity is wrapped up in "elemental poverty," as he puts it. In sabbath time we get to know ourselves as we are. And with that comes great self-compassion. Sabbath gives us perspective. It reconnects us with our imagination. We can envision new ways in which the world might work. "Sabbath is not simply the pause that refreshes. It is the pause that transforms," writes theologian Walter Brueggemann.

Sabbath time will look different for each of us. Much depends on the caring responsibilities we have and the rhythm of our lives. But even if we can't be alone, we can come to share time differently by simply creating a small ritual with a candle or a piece of music. We can sing or paint or sleep with a spirit of surrender. We can return to an inwardness, where we befriend our silence and solitude. By keeping a sabbath, we can remember that all is well and that we are part of the invisible kinship of all things. That we are beloved and beautiful. Sabbath helps us connect with ourselves by reminding us that we are profoundly good enough—just as we are.

CHAPTER 2

Connecting with Others

M Y COFOUNDER of Sacred Design Lab Sue Phillips explains that connecting with self is inextricably linked to connecting with others. The question "Who am I?" leads inevitably to "Whose am I?" because who we understand ourselves to be is inherently shaped by the people we're in relationship with. This chapter explores how we can translate ancient practices that help us be more human together, how to deepen the quality of the relationships we already have, and perhaps how to open doors to new connections also.

Research promises us that this is what makes life meaningful. The Harvard Study of Adult Development, which began amid the Great Depression in 1938, has tracked over seven hundred men, and sometimes their spouses, to understand what makes a life of health and happiness. After eighty years of research, the scientists concluded that the quality of participants' relationships with their friends, families, and partners mattered most. Researchers collected all sorts of data. Every few years, research staff gathered medical records and brain scan data and interviewed the participants about various elements of their lives. In later years, researchers also talked to participants' spouses and children and filmed their daily interactions at home.

Robert Waldinger, clinical professor of psychiatry at Harvard Medical School, who is the fourth person to lead the research team over the decades, explains three key conclusions from the study. First, social connections are good for us. With one in five Americans saying they are lonely, relationships with our family, friends, and broader community help us live longer and happier lives. Second, it is not so much the number of relationships in our life, but their quality, that matters most. Living in the midst of conflict is deeply destructive for our health, while living in the midst of warm relationships is protective. When researchers looked back at the data collected decades ago, they discovered that cholesterol levels were less indicative of health and happiness than the rate of satisfaction in relationships. "The people who were the most satisfied in their relationships at age 50 were the healthiest at age 80," explains Waldinger. On the days when they had more physical pain, older people in satisfying relationships were just as happy as they were on the days when they felt fine. But for the elderly participants who had unsatisfying relationships, their physical pain was magnified by emotional pain. Finally, the study concluded that good relationships don't just protect our bodies; they protect our brains. When we feel like we can count on other people in times of need, our memory stays intact for longer.

Waldinger, outside his day job as a scientist, is also a Zen priest. His research has deeply influenced his own life. "It's easy to get isolated," he explains, "to get caught up in work and not remembering, 'Oh, I haven't seen these friends in a long time,' so I try to pay more attention to my relationships than I used to."

And those kinds of warm relationships need tending. As we've seen, our tech often gets in the way. Writing for UC Berkeley's *Greater Good* magazine, developmental pediatrician Mark Bertin explains that using social media "can diminish our self-esteem, increase our anxiety and depression, and, paradoxically, make us feel more socially isolated." Instead, we need other ways to create communion with others. Many people struggle with this: there's a growing number of books and articles about loneliness and the crisis of belonging, as I surveyed in the introduction. A 2018 study of twenty thousand Americans revealed that 27 percent rarely or never feel as though there are people who really understand them, while only around half have meaningful in-person social interactions on a daily basis, such as having an extended conversation with a friend or spending quality time with family.

Yet many people have found ways to cultivate connections with others that are meaningful and add up to what Waldinger identified as "the good life." In our research for *How We Gather*, we found two consistent community-building trends: people getting together to eat, and people getting together to work out. This chapter draws on ancient practices of creating rituals at mealtime and being aware of our bodies to deepen these daily activities of bonding with others as spiritual practices.

Eating Together as a Sacred Practice

Lennon Flowers's mother was diagnosed with cancer when Lennon was a high school senior. Four years later, she died—just as Lennon was finishing her last year of college. Originally from North Carolina, Lennon eventually moved to Los Angeles and found that she had few ways to talk about her mom and the life she'd lived, about how her influence had shaped the person Lennon had become, and how her mom's absence complicated her family story. "I didn't know how to bring it into a conversation without scaring off new friends," Lennon explains. When asked about plans for Mother's Day or Thanksgiving, the conversation would end awkwardly. "It was a conversation killer."

Lennon longed to be with people who understood her experience. So in late 2010, Lennon and her friend (and eventual cofounder), Carla Fernandez, hosted a dinner in the backyard of their shared house. Connected by one social degree of separation, this group of twentysomethings found what they were looking for in one another: people who could validate the intensity and significance of an experience. Around this table, with these people, they were able to use their experience to springboard into richer, more honest, and more openhearted lives.

This was the founding of the Dinner Party, one of my favorite communities that we studied in *How We Gather*. The group of friends started to get together every month. Soon, five became six, and not long after, friends and friends of friends were asking to join. New table hosts started bringing people together in San Francisco, Washington, DC, and New York City. Today, there are two-hundred-and-seventy tables all meeting regularly in ninety-five cities and towns worldwide, and all of them meet for dinner. Usually, each guest brings a homemade dish or an item of food, often one that reminds them of their lost loved one. And because everyone in the group is living life after loss, no topic is off the table. They can be honest about their anger and relief as much as the sadness they feel. And as time passes, the immediate overwhelm of grief melts into a life where grief has its place alongside joy. Work struggles and promotions, new relationships, family challenges—all of these are welcome at the table.

There is no better way to build community than to eat together. For millennia, humans have shared food. First they did so out of biological necessity by sharing the spoils of gathering and hunting, and later as an expression of kinship. By sharing the same bowl, potential rivals could demonstrate that neither would poison the other. Legend has it that this is also why we clink glasses before a meal. If, as our glasses or tankards touch, the liquid inside skips over from one into another, we can all be assured of our safety! Eating together has always been how we've done community. It's a space and set time to be together, and the act of eating provides interruptions that move conversation organically or help temper awkward introductions. Filmmaker Nora Ephron, who directed my beloved *You've Got Mail*, famously wrote, "A family is a group of people who eat the same thing for dinner."

Some of the most important religious rituals center on shared eating or drinking. Think of the Japanese tea ceremony inspired by Zen Buddhist tradition. Or the Sikh langar, a community meal where all strata of society eat together, no matter caste or creed. Muslims break their fast at the end of the day during Ramadan with an iftar, or evening meal. And of course, the center of the Christian liturgical tradition is the celebration of the Eucharist, or Lord's Supper. Though the typical nibble of wafer and sip of wine are far from the actual meal the ritual reenacts, let's draw out some of the lessons that this tradition offers for shared eating as a sacred practice.

By sitting down together, we signal that we need one another. Orthodox Christian theologian Alexander Schmemann writes that "to eat is still something more than to maintain bodily functions. People may not understand what that 'something more' is, but they nonetheless desire to celebrate it." Schmemann offers insight for us as we create our own sacred eating practice: he argues that something reverential happens when we share a meal. This may sound abstract, but his reason for this makes sense when you understand that it is based in an uncommon interpretation of traditional Communion liturgy in which Christians receive the body and blood of Christ. Theologians tend to focus on what happens to the food: Does it *become* Jesus's body? Or does it merely *symbolize* it? But Schmemann doesn't ask those questions. Instead, he writes in his book *For the Life of the World* that "we must understand that what 'happens' to bread and wine happens because something has, first of all, happened to us." It is because *we* have gathered together—in Schmemann's understanding, as a church community—that the bread and wine have changed. In this sacred time together, he writes, "we . . . are standing beyond time and space."

Can you hear the echo of Heschel's idea here: that the sabbath is a palace in time? In the same way, a sacred practice draws us out of our everyday habits and into a deeper presence. In this case, our presence is with the people around us. And that's what happens at the Dinner Party. Eating together allows a deeper experience of connection. "We know how to be together around a table," explained Lennon when we spoke on the phone. "Walking into a room with chairs in a circle for a facilitated conversation is always going to feel stiffer than sitting down for dinner and passing the salad to your neighbor. Over dinner, you can chat happily to the person next to you, or pick up your fork if you don't want to say a word." And for those who have lost loved ones to cancer, as Lennon has, there's extra resonance in eating together. "I think about my mom's loss of appetite during chemo. It wasn't just hard for her physically, she had this huge social loss of not being able to share meals with her friends." Eating together affirms the simple fact of being alive.

This shared practice has changed Lennon's understanding of the Dinner Party community itself. Yes, it's a community that gathers around the experience of grief. But that's not actually what it's for. Grief was an experience that disconnected people. And the Dinner Party is a modern ritual that overcomes that disconnection and helps people reconnect. Lennon's team noticed this after hosts started to receive notes asking if a pet's death, or an estrangement, or surviving sexual violence "counted" as loss for the Dinner Party community. "We realized," explains Lennon, "that we're not exclusively a vehicle for connecting around grief from death or loss, but for taking sources of struggle and turning them into experiences of connectivity." The Dinner Party has even launched an umbrella organization to help share their principles and methodologies with others looking to build meaningful community around isolating subjects. The dinner table was their alchemic cauldron, transforming suffering into connection.

The Dinner Party is no longer just a small regular gathering in Los Angeles: it is a worldwide community with ordinary people creating meaningful connections with one another. Participants can "join a table" or become a regular host, and this organic community-building has established a powerful space to gather and heal together.

A RITUAL BEFORE WE EAT

Not every dinner is going to be like this. And it's totally fine for most meals to be more perfunctory! (And to be honest, now and then, sitting in front of YouTube is exactly what we need.) Dinner parties of all shapes and sizes can be community-building and nurturing, from regular potlucks to book clubs to game night. But when we do want to experience a sacred meal, how do we set that kind of intention? And how do we make sure we're not the only one showing up with that hope for deeper connection? This is where we draw on the traditions of blessing and ritual.

When I was a child, whenever my family sat down together at the kitchen table for dinner, we took one another's hands and sang a simple melody:

> Blessings on the blossom, blessings on the fruit,
> Blessings on the leaf and stem, blessings on the root.
> Blessings on the meal, and peace upon the earth.

Perhaps your family also has a blessing, prayer, or simple words of gratitude that are said before everyone starts to eat. At special mealtimes like Thanksgiving, even those who don't have much ritual in their home life will share a few words of thanks before digging in. A small ritual can transform the table. Simply looking into one another's eyes, raising a glass, and saying "It's good to be together!" reminds us that there's nothing more to do than delight in one another's company. Or you might choose to simply light candles in silence or hold hands for a few seconds, giving everyone a moment of quiet before the eating begins.

Anthropologist Clifford Geertz famously wrote, "In a ritual, the world as lived and the world as imagined . . . turn out to be the same world." In other words, ritual invites us to enter a way of life that we may barely glimpse, to be transported into a future that is simultaneously filled with our intention and yet remains delightfully unpredictable. This is the power of a short ritual moment before eating. It re-centers our attention on one another—our interconnectivity. Ideally, that emphasis on relationship then also stretches beyond those gathered around the table by noticing our dependence on the people who have sown, grown, picked, sorted, and transported the food. We connect through the food chain and offer our thanks to the many hands who made the meal possible.

Whenever we had guests, my mother would add to our short blessing song, "And welcome Amsterdam!" (or whatever city or town our guests were from). As we grew older, my sisters and I would groan in embarrassment. But now, when we gather with our partners and children, though we might experience a strong hint of irony as we reach for one another's hands, by the end of the song we're glad to have blessed the meal and one another. The first few times you practice a new ritual might seem countercultural, but a few words, simply repeated over your meals, can become stitched into the fabric of your family or friendship.

Even when you eat alone, you can use food to connect with

others through the power of imagination that Geertz mentions. Before taking your first bite, notice the colors and smell of your food. Then, as you bring the food to your mouth, notice your body responding: the saliva in your mouth, the hunger in your belly. Finally, as you take the first bite, savor the taste and offer gratitude for the deliciousness to each of the people you imagine have helped provide this food. With each bite, try to send goodwill to each of the people you imagine.

The Necessity of Repetition

Though having a one-off meal with strangers can be intimate and stimulating, the real transformative power of communities like the Dinner Party is the growth of relationships over time. "We have so many rehearsed stories about who we are," says Lennon. "And the true story that we told about ourselves six months ago may no longer be true today. We need one another to help us reexamine the words coming out of our mouth, to reflect on what is happening with our bodies and spirits." With time, we form real relationships where there's nothing to hide. Where one another's presence alone communicates the love and affection we have for one another.

One shorthand for this type of affection is the alchemy of time plus proximity. For three years, Sean and I lived as proctors—a fancy title for a residence assistant—in Harvard University's freshmen dorms. In four hundred square feet, above the room where John F. Kennedy got started, we lived next to twenty-eight teens as they navigated their first year of college. Of course, there were one or two parties that needed to be calmed down, and plenty of conversations about which classes to take, but most of our efforts supported students in building meaningful relationships. Our job was helping students make friends in the first weeks of class, navigating inevitable roommate conflicts, and celebrating the accomplishments and mourning the tragedies that come with life on campus. But most important, we brought the freshmen together every week over food. With themes like "Breakfast for dinner," where we indulged in homemade pancakes and eggs deep into the night, or "Guac-off," where we tested out various guacamole recipes, it was always the evenings when we made food together that bonded the group most successfully. By the end of the year, the students who had invested in relationships—going for meals together, staying in to share stories with one another—were the ones who left for the summer feeling most connected.

In her 2008 commencement address, that's exactly what novelist Barbara Kingsolver urged Duke's graduating class to remember, especially as they set out into a postcollege world where living structures look very different. Looking out over former students and parents, she reflects, "You've been living so close to your friends, you didn't have to ask about their problems, you had to step over them to get into the room! As you moved from dormitory to apartment to whatever . . . you've had such a full life, surrounded by people, in all kinds of social and physical structures, none of which belonged entirely to you. You're told that's all about to change. That growing up means leaving the herd, starting up the long escalator to isolation. Not necessarily. As you leave here, remember what you loved most in this place. Not [Organic Chemistry], I'm guessing, or the crazed squirrels or even the bulk cereal . . . I mean the way you lived, in close and continuous contact. This is an ancient human social construct that once was common in this land. We called it a community."

The irony is that in contexts where we're pushed to be together, whether a dormitory or military basic training, we form relationships that don't even need to be friendships. In dining halls all over the country, by eating together over and over again, we learn that we don't have to like a person in order to love them. Cooking together, sitting down at a table to eat together, especially when that happens again and again over time, is the best way to create that kind of close continuous contact.

KEEPING KOSHER

I am fascinated by religious dietary laws. At first, they seem restrictive, a relic from a bygone era. But what interests me isn't so much which particular foods are forbidden, but rather how creating rules about what, and with whom, to eat can hold communities together.

As anyone who has prepared a meal for a group with multiple dietary needs knows, it can be a tall order to make dinner work for a mix of guests who are vegan, gluten-free, paleo, and lactose-intolerant. As a vegetarian, I know that it is much simpler for me to hang out with other vegetarians. No annoying questions about where I get my protein and no wafts of roast chicken. It makes sense that households or friend groups tend to share the same diet.

Think of the Jewish body of dietary laws, kashrut. Broadly defined, these rules forbid eating shellfish and anything with cloven hooves that doesn't chew the cud—so, no pork. And there's to be no mixing of meat and dairy in the same dish or at the same table. Throughout history, this made eating with others difficult, so to observe religious laws, Jews ate with their own community. And despite centuries of violent oppression and forced relocation, these rules have survived. In some sense, they have transcended their original religious context; even among those who describe themselves as culturally Jewish (rather than religious), many will talk about food as the key marker of their Jewish identity!

What if we reimagine dietary laws in the context of our flaky friends, busy partners, and frequently frustrating family? Imagine if we deepened our haphazard gatherings and dinners to become solid commitments, observing the rule of eating with the same group of friends every Thursday night. Or tried to expand our capacity for relationship by having lunch with our least favorite colleague once a month. In other words, though we don't need to declare which foods we can or can't eat, we should repurpose a model of committing to *those we eat with*.

While we don't need a similar diet to force us to show up (though it probably helps if you have a group of like-eating vegans, paleo diet followers, or simply a group of people that always want pizza after work), we do benefit from this model of regular mealtimes together because it holds us accountable to the relationships we value most. This practice means sitting down together even when we're tired or in a bad mood, when we're new and know it will be awkward, or when we've had a fight with the one we love. It means accepting that some gatherings will be boring or unpleasant and that we have to keep sitting down. Think of this as a reimagined Whole30. Instead of paying attention to carbs and proteins, we're paying attention to whom we should invite to our table. Imagine making the commitment to have someone who needs community over every Sunday night. Is there someone who's just had a breakup? Or lost a job? Or has good news to celebrate? Even if you've moved to a new city, you can invite the person you met on the subway or your Uber driver, the couple who live downstairs or the clerk at the supermarket. This is how eating together can become a sacred practice.

If we're bold, I'd hazard to say that this reimagining of religious dietary law as a catalyst for an established eating time together can still claim the blessing of tradition. Rabbi Abraham Joshua Heschel wrote, "Perhaps the essential message of Judaism is that in doing the finite we may perceive the infinite. It is incumbent on us to obtain the perception of the impossible in the possible, the perception of life eternal in everyday deeds." In eating together, we are reminded of our intrinsic connectedness and the dependence we have on those around us. The food on our plate doesn't need to symbolize anything more than what it is; it is a "language of care," as author Shauna Niequist puts it.

BUILDING RELATIONSHIPS THROUGH FITNESS COMMUNITIES

Eating together is a tried and tested method for connecting deeply with others. And so is our second practice: sweating together. Over and over again in our *How We Gather* research, Angie and I came across communities that focused on embodied practices to build the feeling of belonging. As I explained in this book's introduction, our close study of CrossFit was the gateway example that helped me understand how potent so-called secular, everyday rituals represent an enormous cultural and spiritual shift.

Take, for example, Afro Flow Yoga in Boston, which "promotes healing, balance, peace and the elevation of all humanity through the practices of yoga, dance, rhythms, spirituality and cultural values of the African Diaspora." Founders Leslie Salmon Jones and Jeff Jones explain that practitioners get together to move their bodies but also to build community. When I participated, we all gathered together in a circle before the workout started to share a few words of introduction and intention. What struck me was the sharing part: many yoga classes invite participants to set an intention but rarely ask them to tell the group what it is. In contrast, Afro Flow Yoga embraces the sharing to foster relationship-building from mat to mat, and Leslie and Jeff have that warm presence that invites everyone to feel that they are welcome. They've designed the experience of Afro Flow Yoga not only to connect with one another but also to connect across time to elders and ancestors.

Inspired by Pan-African leader Marcus Garvey's words that "a people without the knowledge of their past history, origin, and culture is like a tree without roots," Leslie and Jeff's work actively contributes to healing generational trauma, especially that of those whose ancestors survived the Middle Passage, where African people were forcefully taken from their homes and enslaved. You can recognize then that the purpose of Afro Flow Yoga is much deeper than simply staying in shape. It is a workout of the heart, a working through of story. It is the work of communal healing.

Similarly, the Nerdstrong Gym in Los Angeles is about much more than bulking or shredding. It got started in a small garage where friends got together to work out and then play games like Dungeons and Dragons. Founder Andrew Deutsch explains on their website: "One day, we turned around and had 15 people show up. That's when we decided to open our own space and see if we could turn a couple of nerds working out into Nerdstrong. Here we are, a few years later, after an expansion of our space, with 2,000 sq ft, lots of weights and one of the best communities ever created." At Nerdstrong, workouts are enriched by weaving sci-fi and fantasy stories into the physical movements. The Boss Monster workout program, for example, is for you if you've ever wanted to try fighting Thanos, defeating Dr. Wily, or taking down Voldemort. Andrew explains: "I always felt like my job . . . was to be available to those that fitness has forgotten about. The nerds. The geeks. So, Nerdstrong is for [them]."

Breaking Through the Vulnerability Barrier

What both these communities demonstrate is the potential for us to use physical exercise to deepen our connection with one another. Both offer bonding, shared experience, and a safe place to be yourself (even if that means fighting a Marvel villain). Dr. Jennifer Carter, the director of sport psychology at Ohio State University's Wexner Medical Center, has explained that "our bodies can hold tension and negative emotions that can be released during physical activity." Our emotional brain is less inhibited when we're exhausted, meaning that high-intensity workouts can give us a powerful emotional release. This, then, is the first practice that we can deepen through exercise: breaking down our vulnerability barriers. Many of us have become hardened cynics as we travel through the world. We don't allow ourselves the joy (and danger) of letting down our guard and allowing others in. Working out together can help. And nowhere did we see this more than at SoulCycle.

At the very beginning of our research, my Divinity School

classmate Zoe Jick invited Angie Thurston and me to come to a SoulCycle class. Though training to become a secular Jewish scholar, Zoe explained that "SoulCycle is my religion." We showed up at the pristine storefront with women in various chic outfits and branded athletic gear. The staff welcomed us warmly—a key ingredient of SoulCycle's success. Cofounder Elizabeth Cutler later explained in a class at Harvard Divinity School that in the early days, when SoulCycle was a small studio hidden away down a dingy corridor on West 72nd Street in New York City, the way they built community was "by loving people into staying." More than a decade later, the mission remains the same: bringing soul to the people. The website reads, "Our one of a kind, rockstar instructors guide riders through an inspirational, meditative fitness experience that's designed to benefit the body, mind and soul. Set in a dark candlelit room to high-energy music, our riders move in unison as a pack to the beat and follow the signature choreography of our instructors. The experience is tribal. It's primal. It's fun." During the forty-five-minute class, riders are united in their physical movement, with each person rotating their wheels to match the beats of the music. It's as much a dance class as a spin class, with shoulders dropping and backsides lifting off the seat in sync with the rest of the room.

All in the name of research, Angie and I tried classes at SoulCycle studios around the country. In West Hollywood, we rode with Angela Davis, a former All-American track athlete and all-star instructor. I was amazed to see that, unlike most instructors, she didn't ride a bike herself; she simply walked among us riders, sharing her soulful message for the day. It's no surprise that Davis is a skilled preacher—she was an undergraduate student at Oral Roberts University, a well-known evangelical Christian university in Oklahoma. "There's a blessing waiting for you on this bike! Go and get it!" she proclaimed. "Angels are clapping for you!" I looked around, astonished at this religious language. Surely this was too much for our spiritual-but-not-religious and secular liberal elite? No. Everyone was cheering, smiling, and grimacing purposefully, pushing harder. Slowly, I allowed myself to experience the ride, not just monitor what others made of it. "Today is the day where you recognize that your dream is valid. It's already in you! It's already been downloaded in your DNA. The capacity to be what you are called, created, and destined to be is in you!" Soon, I was putty in her hands. "*Yes!*" I felt my body saying. "I can do this. I am going to claim what is waiting for me!"

With sweat dripping off my forehead, my mind went quiet, and I began to feel part of something bigger than myself. It was as if my fellow riders and I were part of a larger collective—all moving together. I felt stronger, emboldened by the others around me. The shouts of encouragement from the front, echoed by the riders themselves, powered all of us on. No single part of this bigger cohesive body wanted to let another part down. This is what Zoe had described. That's why she called it her religion.

After thirty-five minutes of high-energy cycling, we got to the hill climb. This is the penultimate song where the beats slow down and the resistance on the bike gets turned up. All the stress and anxiety, the fear and doubt, were melting off us. There we were, raw, fully human in this shared moment of soulful sweat. In nearly every class, this is when the tears come forth. Often riders can't explain what it is they're crying about, but the tears suddenly appear. Nothing is more indicative of a community taking shape than people feeling free to cry in front of one another. This is what makes exercise a powerful connector, even among strangers—our bodies are doing the speaking. In a culture that values rationality and dismisses emotion as untrustworthy, it has become difficult to access our vulnerable core through words and thoughts alone. And especially in public. But with our senses overwhelmed with loud music and darkness, the physical exertion breaks through the barriers we maintain, leaving us open to real connection.

West African spiritual teacher and writer Malidoma Patrice Somé explains that before beginning a ritual, you own the journey. You are in control. But "once the ritual begins, the journey owns you." Somé argues that the lack of modern rituals in the West is in large part because many of us have an overwhelming desire to be in control, which is antithetical to ritual. "To surrender the sense of control can be terrifying." Yet that's exactly what spaces like SoulCycle offer: an experience of surrender. The ritual takes control over the riders. And the crying happens to instructors too! Willie Holmes explained in a video interview, "I've been an instructor for less than two months, but I've cried at least three times. I don't even know why. I wasn't sad or angry or bothered or anything like that;

there were just tears. It's happened in class, after class, while in training. I've never been like that in my whole entire life."

We may come into a workout feeling the anxiety and stress, pressure and pain of everyday life. Exercising together can reset us in our own bodies, but also as part of a collective body. We remember our togetherness. We learn empathy for another's experience. We have the sense of being part of a bigger group, with others who have the full spectrum of emotions and worries as we do.

"Community Is Built Through Suffering and Laughter"

Once we're in that raw, more emotionally available heart space, we're able to more deeply reflect on life's big questions together. Often SoulCycle instructors will ask questions of their riders: "Who are you riding for today?" or "What are you ready to let go of?" Questions like these help us all make meaning of the physical suffering we feel: "I'm riding for my kids," perhaps, or "I'm riding for Neha, who has just been diagnosed with breast cancer." The real trick is to share those reflections together. At CrossFit, workouts will often involve a partner. Each pair may have to complete 150 burpees, and between the two partners, they figure out whether to split the burpees evenly or whether the stronger partner takes on a hundred and the other fifty, for example. At their best, they both share a few words of intention before they start, to elevate the practice to something more meaningful. One CrossFit community in upstate New York run by Lauren and Michael Plank has integrated Bible study, discussion, and prayer into a Friday night workout. Michael explains, "We use CrossFit to help people learn how to take care of themselves . . . how to bond in community, and how to become part of something bigger than themselves. This kind of fitness tests your body, for sure. But it's a huge psychological challenge. And because you're doing it around a bunch of other people, all of these walls come down." Greg Glassman, cofounder of CrossFit, likes to say that real community is built through shared suffering and laughter.

Another prime example of this kind of group meaning-making exercise is the team obstacle course event, Tough Mudder, in which about 500,000 people participate every year. Tough Mudder creates obstacles that incorporate three themes: strength (obstacles that are difficult), fear (obstacles that look harrowing), and teamwork (obstacles that an individual alone cannot surmount). One obstacle that relies on teamwork is the Block Ness Monster. Made of a large pool of water, over a meter deep, with a large rotating block in the middle of it, racers have to coordinate with one another to successfully rotate the block in order to cross the water. My friend Rabbi Elan Babchuk gets together with a group of college friends every year to run a Tough Mudder. Their team is humorously called "Mountain Jew," and the trip has become an annual community ritual that gives him a few days away from work and family responsibilities to check in with beloved old friends in a way that goes much deeper than a few hours together or a random phone call.

"We trained together as a team for months leading up to the Tough Mudder, running up the steepest hills in Rhode Island during ungodly hours so that the first moment of standing at the foot of the ski mountain wouldn't be so daunting come race day. By the time we were on the course, the mere act of overcoming frightening obstacles together and running for five hours gave us plenty of opportunities to connect much more deeply than we otherwise would have. By hour 3 on the course you've faced your fear of heights, considered your mortality, and crawled through mud and barbed wire together as a team, and all the normal barriers to meaningful connection have been stripped away. The conversations shift from commentary on the obstacles to reflections on life, and the shift is seamless."

The Tough Mudder experience is designed to physically connect you in some unusual and challenging ways. Elan explains, "By the time you get to the Electroshock Therapy at the finish line," where dozens of live wires hang over mud from a wooden frame, "and lock your arms together in order to dilute the impending shock, you feel like you've gone through a complete transformation—as an individual and as a group of friends."

Of course, similar principles apply to a hiking or pickup basketball group, or going on a long dog walk with a friend or neighbor. The key is to find a way to reflect on meaningful questions together during or straight after a shared, physically challenging experience. So try and recruit a friend, set a time, and then—as with any sacred practice—intentionally start the activity not so much focused on burning calories but on how you can connect with your fellow adventurer. You might ask a question like "What's inspiring you at the moment?" or "Who taught you how to keep going when times are hard?" All this will have the added halo effect that, down the line, your running buddy might become a friend who brings over food when you're nursing or sick. And if you're connecting with an instructor or group fitness leader, you might ask them to officiate life-transition moments like a wedding! There are already countless stories of SoulCycle instructors, for example, offering ritual leadership for their faithful flock.

Decentering Yourself

The final practice to explore through fitness is the process of decentering yourself and focusing on a larger, connected collective. A 2012 study by Russell Hoye, Matthew Nicholson, and Kevin Brown showed that even a low degree of involvement in team sport was associated with increased social connectedness for individuals. Though the most obvious examples are team sports like soccer, you might also recognize that feeling if you've ever had help moving house—forming a human chain, carrying endless boxes back and forth. Or crossing turbulent water while white-water rafting, getting down in a Zumba class, or letting loose on the dance floor. When we're in the rhythm of the collective, we can be freed of our isolationist perspective. For a brief period of time, the lie of our separateness is exposed, and we remember that we are wholly connected to one another. It's not that our individuality disappears, but that we are no longer blinded by individualism. That's why finding an exercise community can foster a sense of belonging that replicates what religious groups once did. Think of congregations singing together or the Sufi tradition of whirling together.

One fitness community that has taken the practice of decentering oneself seriously is the November Project. In particular, they've created a culture of accountability whereby participants start to move from showing up for themselves to showing up on behalf of one another. It all started in 2011, when cofounders Brogan Graham and Bojan Mandaric, both Northeastern University crew alumni, made a commitment to each other to work out every single day at 6:30 a.m. through the cold month of November. The habit stuck, and quickly friends began to join. What started in Boston has now grown to forty-nine cities around the world. Showing up for one another is at the core of what makes November Project work, because who really wants to meet in the rain, cold, or even snow at 6:30 a.m. to run up and down stadium steps?

The November Project has developed two key rituals for participants so they can keep putting one another at the center and keep one another honest. Each week a ceremonial stick, known as the Positivity Award, is given to the person who has most benefited the community and the wider city. Made from a sawn-off rowing oar, it symbolizes the sometimes difficult-to-see work of steering a boat, shifting direction, or doing some extra paddling to keep everyone afloat. Every time it is awarded, the recipient receives huge cheers and hugs from the tens, or hundreds, of people who have shown up. Often there are tears of joy and appreciation.

But the carrot of motivation is only one side of the story. If friends promise one another that they'll show up but then break their word, their names are listed publicly on the website with a note of (loving) accountability. One example from New York includes multiple pictures of Mary, who didn't show, and reads, "Mary, last night you dropped a verbal [commitment] to Aliza via text that you would meet her to run together to the workout. As she stood cold, wet, and sad at your door step you never came out from your comfy warm bed. . . . I guess what the tribe is saying is that WE MISSED YOU TODAY!!!! Today was just a little drearier because we didn't have your bright shiny face on this rainy gloomy day."

These tools are nothing new, though perhaps posting pictures on an organizational home page is. Social reputation has been a driver for congregational attendance in communities for centuries. It represented the commitment to the whole, rather than the interests of an individual. Though congregational gathering served the purpose of worshipping God, that in itself served a sociological function of decentering individuals and centering something greater. This transcendent and communal focus allows group tasks to succeed, like harvesting crops, constructing barns, raising children, and burying the dead. The November Project, where especially active groups meet three times a week, offers a somewhat congregational lifestyle that is grounded in the ethos of depending on one another. The Positivity Award and tongue-in-cheek accountability blog posts are simply tools that stave off selfishness and ennoble the connection to one another.

In all these decentering practices, it's important to note that a strong community should not deny one's individuality. That's when communities become cults. Among the fitness groups profiled here, the continued personalization is visible in how participants set their own speed or weight or intensity of the workout, for example. Though there may be a unifying consistency of running up and down the stadium steps, at the November Project there's an option of doing half the steps, running up and down the whole stadium from right to left, or for the particularly ambitious, doing that and back again. At Soul-Cycle, riders are in charge of their own resistance dial, meaning everyone can set their own workout intensity. Instructors may invite them to "crank it up," but the final choice remains with each individual. This is the guiding principle of a healthy, meaningful fitness community: a community can flourish only when each individual member flourishes. Nobody is forced to surrender their identity or level of skill and confidence.

Of course, the November Project, Tough Mudder, SoulCycle, and CrossFit are just a few data points on a much larger map. From double dutch meet-ups and cheerleading to triathlons, from Spartan Race and Orangetheory to Jelly Fam on the basketball court, the rave culture of the 1990s, and the underground ballroom scene—each activity helps people connect to one another through an embodied experience. Another fitness-related community Angie and I studied in *How We Gather* that embodied connection with others through movement was dance. Daybreaker and Morning Gloryville, which host early-morning sober raves, were two unexpected groups that showed how people are engaging with traditionally mystical practices in secular spaces. Gathering with fruit juices before work, hundreds of millennials dance wildly to great music, all completely sober. Fitness is part of the draw, but mostly it's about joyfulness. Participants describe feeling inspired and energized as their bodies release a heady mix of dopamine and other feel-good chemicals. While traveling to learn folk music through the region of Svaneti, in the Caucasus country of Georgia, I felt the same rush of connection while taking part in traditional circle dances. Indeed, Aldous Huxley famously saw dance as particularly important to human culture. Sacred dance has ancient roots, from Hinduism to Shintoism to indigenous Native American traditions, and was used as prayer or to reenact myths. "Ritual dances provide a religious experience that seems more satisfying and convincing than any other," Huxley wrote. "It is with their muscles that humans most easily obtain knowledge of the divine."

PREPARE YOURSELF: COMMUNITY IS WONDERFUL AND TERRIBLE

But as we build connections to others, heed this warning from the wise community-builders who have come before us—in particular, my hero Jean Vanier. He was the founder of L'Arche, a global network of communities in which people with intellectual disabilities, and those who assist them, live together, sharing life under one roof. Rather than thinking of care as a client-centered model, L'Arche and other groups like the Camphill Movement put the community at the center and give everyone responsibility to serve one another. This means that everyone contributes in whatever ways they can. For staff, that means doing their jobs—accounting, cleaning, caring, planning visit days, and so on—but also putting together theatrical performances and leading songs. For L'Arche members with learning disabilities, it means working in the gardens, preparing meals, welcoming guests, laying the table, or baking bread to sell. Everyone cares for one another, dignifying one another and the wider community.

Volunteers come from all over the world to live and work in L'Arche communities, wanting, at first, to help those who are disabled. This is a noble instinct and one I recognize immediately. I had the same instinct as a teenager, wanting to help those in need (or think of Hermione as she seeks to help house-elves in the Harry Potter books). But the L'Arche movement is clear that this instinct is only half the story. By living alongside those whose needs are so evident and who are often so startlingly transparent about their desire for connection by spontaneously giving hugs or constantly wanting conversation, new volunteers are confronted by their own vulnerability and deep desires for love and belonging.

In one of the most important texts I've read, *Community*

and Growth, Vanier writes that when we enter into community we find the warmth of love to be exhilarating. This feeling of welcome allows us to lift our masks and barriers and to become more vulnerable with one another. We enter into a time of communion and great joy. "But then too," he writes, "as [we] lift [our] masks and become vulnerable, [we] discover that community can be a terrible place, because it is a place of relationship; it is the revelation of our wounded emotions and of how painful it can be to live with others, especially with some people. It is so much easier to live with books and objects, televisions, or dogs and cats! It is so much easier to live alone and just do things for others when one feels like it." Sister of Saint Joseph Sue Mosteller, who has spent four decades living in L'Arche communities, puts it very simply: "Community is the most *wonderful* thing in the world. And it is also the most *terrible!*"

THE COURAGE TO DEEPEN OUR CONNECTIONS

"Each person with his or her history of being accepted or rejected, with his or her past history of inner pain and difficulties in relationships with parents, is different," writes Vanier. "But in each one there is a yearning for communion and belonging, but at the same time a fear of it." Though we long for connection and love from others, we also fear it the most. It means taking the risk to be vulnerable and open. We worry that we'll be constricted by the relationships of care, that our creativity will suffer. We want to belong and then fear the little sacrifices that this belonging will demand of us as we make space for others around us. We want to be special. Different. Unique. We fear the discipline and commitment that will be asked of us. But in the moments of loneliness, we know that the cost of staying afraid and disconnected is too great. This is a time for community. A time for connection.

In each of our lives there are connections and communities that can be enriched, deepened: friends we go to the movies with, five-a-side soccer clubs, local parent email lists, neighbors, cousins. Why not take a cue from ancient traditions and choose one of these relationships and commit to hosting six meals for them in the coming year. Or join a community-oriented fitness group or running club. Search the hundreds of thousands of meetups, and choose five near you to check out, even if you go with zero expectation to return. Over dinner with friends, follow Priya Parker's advice in her wonderful book *The Art of Gathering* and cause some "good controversy" by sharing a stimulating, gently provocative idea or story without requiring others to expose themselves emotionally more than they want to. In my experience, nearly every authentic attempt to build community is welcomed. Who knows what delightful connections you'll deepen!

CHAPTER 3

Connecting with Nature

O UR AWARENESS of who we are, and whose we are, is deepened when we connect to the natural world. Surrounded by nature is where we remember what really matters. Our peak experiences give us an overwhelming sense of awe and a momentary taste of the meaning of life. Often it is in nature where we feel a profoundly moving sense that we are connected to everything around us. Being in nature re-centers our priorities away from self-involvement, bitterness, and despair and opens up new possibilities and a greater capacity for compassion. It can even be a central pillar of recovery for those struggling with severe depression. This chapter explores how we can deepen our existing connection to nature so that we feel truly at home in the world. We'll explore three ancient practices: pilgrimage, celebrating the seasons, and reimagining the distinction between our bodies and the outside world.

We urgently need these practices. More than half of the world's population now lives in an urban area, and within thirty years that proportion will be up to almost 70 percent. Already, the average American spends only 7 percent of their time outdoors, according to the results of an Environmental Protection Agency-sponsored survey published in 2001. As we've moved more and more of our lives indoors, especially to work and to be entertained in front of our screens, scientists are warning that we're entering an age of "nature deficit disorder." Coined by Richard Louv, nature deficit disorder describes the human costs of alienation from nature, among them diminished use of the senses, attention difficulties, and higher rates of physical and emotional illnesses.

This is a strange place to be. Our ancestors' lives and systems of meaning-making were fundamentally formed by the natural world around them. The gods they worshipped were deeply shaped by the landscapes they lived in. The rituals they maintained used flora and fauna that were available to them, and the wishes they made were for favorable weather, a strong herd, or a good harvest. It would have been difficult to imagine a separate concept of "nature," so deeply entwined was everyday life with its natural surroundings. Even as cultures urbanized and later industrialized, human beings have continued to celebrate the changing seasons, invoked the language of gardens in their imagination of a divine heaven, and looked to the night sky for guidance through astrology. Today, we can draw on these traditions to enrich our experience of connection to place toward a spiritually fulfilled life.

It's not just religious traditions that are interested in our connection to the natural world. Scientists, too, have concluded that spending time in nature is connected to all sorts of health benefits. The gentle burbling of a brook or the sound of the wind in the trees shifts your nervous system into a relaxed state, according to a 2017 *Scientific Reports* paper, and data reveals that people who have regular access to nature are less likely to be on antidepressants. Expectant mothers who spend time in nature have healthier babies, and being around plants can even strengthen our immune system and prevent illness.

A 2015 study from Stanford University demonstrated that those who took a ninety-minute walk through a natural landscape had reduced neural activity in an area of the brain linked to risk for mental illness compared to those who walked in an urban environment. Other research shows that "forest bathing," the practice of spending time in a forested area, has multiple positive effects on human well-being. So much do city dwellers long for time out in nature that there's a significant growth in organizations like Blackberry Farm in Walland, Tennessee, which runs a Deep Healing Woods program inspired by the Japanese practice of shinrin-yoku, or forest medicine. New companies like Getaway are growing, providing tiny houses in natural settings (with a lockbox to put away your phone). Pitched as an "experience designed to bring us back to our elements, immerse us in the magic of the woods, and challenge us to rediscover the pleasure of boredom, solitude, and unstructured time," it has proved especially popular with young urbanites willing to part with money in exchange for the beauty of natural surroundings. Indeed excuses to get outdoors are increasingly on the minds of young urbanites. Last year the *New York Times* reported that fly-fishing was the latest old-timey hobby to gain a dedicated new following.

I certainly remember forests offering me refuge in times of stress. Growing up in the Ashdown Forest in the southeast of England, our garden backed onto a path that took you into the woodland. At age eight or nine, I would build huts in the bracken and fallen branches. Once, overcome by childhood anger, I packed a bag with a pint of milk, a loaf of bread, and my violin and ran into the forest, planning never to come back. (The violin, I hoped, might bring in some busking money . . .) No surprise, my forest bath calmed me down, and I returned home within the hour.

Though a forest is ideal, even individual trees can move us. You may remember hearing about what happened when the city of Melbourne, Australia, assigned email addresses to trees throughout the city so that citizens could report dangerous branches or other problems. Instead, nearby citizens wrote thousands of love letters to their favorite trees. This one was typical:

Dear Green Leaf Elm,

I hope you like living at St. Mary's. Most of the time I like it too. I have exams coming up and I should be busy studying. You do not have exams because you are a tree. I don't think that there is much more to

talk about as we don't have a lot in common, you being a tree and such.
But I'm glad we're in this together.

Silly, perhaps, but that last phrase—"We're in this together"—
is the kind of connection that the three practices in this chapter are designed to help us remember. We are not separate
from nature, we are nature itself, and we are very much in
this together.

RETRIEVING THE ART OF PILGRIMAGE

Pilgrimages come in all shapes and sizes.

Nearly all of us move from one place to another. We go to
work or school or visit family. We might walk the dog, go for
a hike, or go to our favorite café to pick up the best hot chocolate in town. Now and then, we'll make an effort to travel
somewhere particularly meaningful. We might take a vacation
to visit distant friends, go to the burial place of a loved one,
or see a favorite band or performer in concert. But could these
humble journeys away from our homes form the basis of a
sacred practice? I believe they can. After all, a pilgrimage is
simply a transformative journey on foot to a special or sacred
place. And with some attention, intention, and repetition, we
can deepen some of these journeys to become pilgrimages.

Pilgrimages are grand and arduous in our imagination,
in part because the best-known religious pilgrimages are in
fact grand and arduous! The world's maps are dotted with ancient pilgrim routes. More than 300,000 people from around

the world walk the Camino de Santiago to the shrine of Saint James in northern Spain each year. More than one-hundred-and-twenty million Hindus traveled across India in 2013 for the Kumbh Mela festival to bathe in the sacred river Ganges. But perhaps the best-known pilgrimage today is the hajj, which nearly two million Muslims complete every year, following in the footsteps of the Prophet Muhammad. The journey is a sacred obligation for all Muslims who are able to travel and is designed to promote the bonds of unity across geography and social status. However, the pilgrimages in our lives can be as big or small as we need. A pilgrimage isn't defined by distance, but by transformation. I love anthropologists Victor and Edith Turner's definition of pilgrimage sites like Mecca and Medina as places where miracles are believed to have happened, still happen, and may happen again.

Pilgrimages of any scale follow the same broad architecture with three phases. The first is the setting of a purpose or intention. This might be healing, marking a loss, asking for forgiveness, exploring a new life phase or transition, or simply reconnecting with joy. It might even be simply the intention of adventure—creating space in which unexpected new thoughts, friendships, or experiences might emerge.

The second phase is the journey itself. The hours spent walking, the blisters, the stunning views, the incessant rain or burning sun. The drudgery and then startling moments of magic. The conversations with fellow travelers along the road. In the final phase, the arrival and return, we integrate what we've experienced on the road back into our own lives. We frame a photograph from the journey, we tell stories about the adventures we had. Maybe we seek out a regular chance to be outside, having spent time among the elements.

Will Parsons and Guy Hayward, cofounders of the British Pilgrimage Trust, know all about the ancient art of pilgrimage. Will, in particular, has discovered all the old secrets of a good sacred journey because he is a modern-day troubadour. He has been walking through the back lanes and forest paths of Britain for fifteen years, camping in the woods and singing for his supper. "You can make pilgrimage anytime," he says, "along a Great Route or from your back door." I joined Will and Guy on a daylong pilgrimage in the countryside surrounding Oxford, England, back in 2016. We set off on foot from the town center, leaving behind the busy streets and following the river Thames north to our destination: a twelfth-century church outside the village of Binsey. Our intention was simple—after a few days working together in a conference room, we wanted to stretch our legs. Soon, the bustle of tourists and town was behind us, and instead we contended with various brambles and weeds in the hedgerow along the path.

Walking, instead of driving or even cycling, brings us into an easy rhythm with the landscape around us. My friend and Episcopal priest Marisa Egerstrom likes to say this is traveling "at the speed of sniffs." Just like an enthusiastic dog on the road, we notice all sorts of interesting sights and smells that invite further investigation. Our breath slows down. We become present.

Pilgrimage is a multisensory experience. It's about making

contact, getting up close and touching, looking, smelling, listening, even tasting the land around us. Indeed, a few years after Henry VIII outlawed pilgrimage in England, an injunction forbade any kissing or licking of shrines—a sure sign that this is exactly what people were doing. Clearly, intimacy with the world around us belongs to any pilgrimage! Will encouraged us to eat any berries that we found and had brought a flask of pre-boiled hot water with us so that when we found some dandelion leaves or edible herbs, we could make our own pilgrim tea. "It's just another way of making contact with the world," he explained.

As we walked, Will encouraged us to find a stick—a pilgrim's staff. "Carrying a stick feels right," explained Will. "It's one of our oldest and most important technologies. Think of the importance of other staffs—the scythe, the scepter, the spear, the seed-dibber, the bow, and the fishing rod—and you begin to realize why it feels so natural in your hand." It is also a literal invitation to take nature into our own hands—finding the right length and strength of stick that helps us feel at home as we walk through fields or forest. A staff is the perfect prop; it propels us along, supports our heavy backpacks, and immediately communicates to the world that we're a pilgrim! Plus, we get to impersonate Gandalf.

Pilgrimage is perfect for you if the traditional reflective exercises of journaling and mindfulness fall short. Journalist Karin Klein bluntly explains why walking works for her. "I can't meditate for shit," she writes in *Yes!* magazine. "Sitting that long, paying attention to my breath or an imaginary white light, chafes my natural impatience. In contrast, hiking easily brings me to that sought-after state of being 'in the moment.'" Hikers have to pay attention to where they are and what's going on around them. If they don't, they'll trip or fall afoul of annoyances such as poison oak and poison ivy. "At the same time, the trail is a multisensory experience that calls on us to observe wildflowers, smell aromatic plants, and hear bird calls and the rustle of small animals in the brush." Klein points to the numerous benefits of being outdoors—exposure to the color green has been shown to be relaxing and calming, for example. Pilgrimage might also be right for you if you find yourself without words to describe what you're going through. We can walk, rather than talk, through our grief. There are various intentional walking groups to support people whose loved ones have died, for example.

Back in Oxfordshire, it wasn't long before our countryside walk led us to our destination, the small church outside the village of Binsey. When we walk a pilgrimage, we tread in the footsteps of many before us, and so the land itself gets wrapped up in story. Will told us the remarkable tale of Frideswide, who is remembered at the church. Born in the seventh century, she founded a priory and was sworn to celibacy. A nearby king, Algar, sought to marry Frideswide, but she refused. Legend has it that the abbess fled to Oxford, where the local people hid her from the raging Algar. As the king searched the town he was struck blind, allowing her to return safely to the priory to live with her nuns. Hundreds of years after her death, during Henry VIII's sacking of the monasteries, Frideswide was once again in danger. As all relics were to be destroyed, the story tells that her bones were thrown into the river. But the people of Oxford, who had protected her once, fished the bones out of the water and saved the saint anew.

Hearing Frideswide's story brought the landscape I was traversing to life. No longer were the fields one monotonous continuity; instead, each presented itself as a player in the drama. The back roads and the river now sparkled with history. Might this be the place her bones were rescued from the river? Might she have hidden in this copse of trees? But you don't need a saint's story to make a landscape come to life. Great stories of love and loss, revenge and regret, are everywhere to be found. Even the most unremarkable suburb is drenched in story. Discovering factual history, family stories, fairytales, or local legends—this is part of pilgrimage, retelling and perhaps reinventing stories that connect our souls to the soil. Filmmaker Phil Cousineau writes that pilgrimage exists to help us "remember the mysteries you forgot at home." The Japanese mendicant poet Matsuo Bashō, famous for his haiku, talks of the "glimpse of the under-glimmer," an experience that lurks beneath the surface of stereotypes and numbness through which we can see the vibrant, deep reality of a living landscape and our own true identity.

When I was a boy, my local choir director embarked on a walk around Britain, literally circumnavigating the whole of the British Isles. The stories he collected from soaring cliffs to industrial estates brought to life the land he lived on. This is how we can bring landscapes back to life, by walking through them and hearing their stories. Vanessa Zoltan, my podcast cohost, leads secular pilgrimages through the landscapes that inspired authors like Louisa May Alcott, Charlotte Brontë, and Virginia Woolf, adding a new dimension of insight into their novels by walking through the land they lived on.

Eventually, my pilgrimage with Will and Guy came to its destination, Saint Margaret's. But the biggest lesson from my pilgrimage wasn't the church. Standing outside Saint Margaret's, we didn't head straight for the church door. Instead, we stopped at an enormous yew tree, itself over three hundred years old, growing next to the church. Its evergreen canopy cast a long shadow and towered above us. Here Will invited us to reconnect with our intention of getting our bodies out of the meeting room and into the wild. Then he instructed us to walk around the tree three times. This seemed strange at first, but it allowed me to admire this magnificent tree from every angle, and by the third time around, I felt as if I had some relationship with this tree and the place in which it stood. I wanted to touch it, and so I went up to its ragged bark-clad trunk and gave it a big hug.

This practice of circumambulation is a key spiritual tool to transform any journey into a pilgrimage. By making repeated circles around our destination, we create a sacred center. Our journey itself honors what we leave in the middle. Think of pilgrims walking around—never up—the sacred Kii Mountains in Japan, dotted with Shinto and Buddhist shrines. Or the Kaaba, the building at the center of Islam's most holy mosque in Mecca, around which pilgrims walk seven times at the end of the hajj. Circumambulation allows us to see every angle of our destination or the object of our veneration.

Finally, Will took us to the spring, bubbling forth next to the yew tree. There we filled our flasks while he sang a blessing for water, the source of life:

> *Water flows, life is given,*
> *Rises from earth, falls from heaven,*
> *Water flowing so we sing*
> *Bless the holy spring.*

As we returned home, I had seen, touched, smelled, heard, and even tasted the landscape we had walked through. No longer was this a postcard view of a genteel English countryside. There was a wildness to it—and a wildness in me that had been reawakened. No longer was I imprisoned by whiteboards and a laptop screen!

With pilgrimage, new possibilities about who we are and where we belong emerge. Walking a pilgrimage is like living a question mark. Everything is new, even when you've seen it before. A walk you've taken before can become a mini pilgrimage if you infuse it with openness to transformation during the experience and a keen, observant attitude. Things get churned up by walking. You wonder. You reminisce. You question. As we connect with forgotten bits of a landscape, we connect with forgotten bits of ourselves too. As pilgrims, we remember how to actually *be* in a place. Malidoma Patrice Somé writes that when we become aware of the home we have in nature, we sense home in whatever place we're in.

Modern pilgrimage not only comes in all shapes and sizes, but it also comes with diverse intentions motivating them. This is why pilgrimage is such a valuable tool for reconnecting with the natural world: the destination and the journey can both be outside church walls. My friend and composer Brendan Taaffe made the commitment many years ago to go for a few days of solo hiking in the mountains every year. And each time, he takes the same book of poetry with him, finds a spot far from any human ears, and reads the entire book aloud to the majestic peaks and rocky crags around him.

Of course, walking alone brings with it safety concerns, especially for women, and so shared pilgrimage is another option to explore. Together with my fellow adventurer Caroline Howe, I traveled to the west coast of Ireland to visit the grave of John O'Donohue, the former priest and poet, about whom I wanted to write my Divinity School thesis. Caroline was recuperating from an ankle injury, and I have fond memories of pushing her up enormous hills in her wheelchair as we enjoyed the soft—ever-present—Irish rain streaking across our faces. I remember picking flowers together to put on his grave, the journey enriched by the fact that we were doing it together.

Pilgrimages are found in all sorts of unlikely shapes and sizes. In our *How We Gather* research, Angie and I came across modern pilgrims through the Millennial Trains Project (MTP), which took cohorts of about twenty young leaders on a cross-country train journey to learn about social entrepreneurship and to see anew smaller cities that have been dismissed as "rust belt" urban areas in decline. MTP helped stitch together the fabric of landscape and city, revealing the hinterlands around the city centers that are so easily forgotten. While it was pilgrimage by train instead of foot, it remained a powerful, spiritually infused journey. When we first interviewed MTP's founder, Patrick Dowd, he was eager to stress the secular nature of the journey. But as our conversation progressed, he mused, "Well, I guess someone did bless the train when we left the station." We cannot help but be changed by our journey and so can come back with new curiosity and care for the landscapes in which we spend most of our time.

Pilgrimage can happen anywhere: a hike in the desert or a walk around the block, solo camping in the Rockies or a family trip to the dog park. What matters is setting an intention before we head out, paying attention to the natural world along the way—using all five senses if possible—and returning home again with a new perspective. Perhaps only at the end of a pilgrimage, after all the preparation and arduous travel, can we speak to how our relationship to nature has changed. Has the landscape spoken to our longing? Have we reconnected with our inner wholeness that we lose so easily in our day-to-day busyness? Have we let ourselves be soothed and tested by the bigger home that we all share?

Permission to Be Creative

It might seem strange to think about a short walk through your neighborhood as a pilgrimage. Using a word like "pilgrimage" can feel like we're taking something traditional and changing it too quickly. This is a mistake. Those religious leaders who rail against change often confuse tradition with convention; they assume that one way of fulfilling a particular purpose is the *only* way of fulfilling it. (Scholar Mark Jordan jests that whenever someone invokes "venerable tradition," they are nearly always referring to what they experienced—or heard about—as a child.) Twentieth-century Trappist monk and writer Thomas Merton wrote insightfully, "Convention and tradition may seem on the surface to be much the same thing. But this superficial resemblance only makes conventionalism all the more harmful. In actual fact, conventions are the death of real tradition as they are of all real life. They are parasites which attach themselves to the living organism of tradition and devour all its reality, turning it into a hollow formality." This is what has happened with so many sacred practices.

"Tradition is living and active," Merton writes, "but convention is passive and dead." While convention is merely accepted passively and lived as a routine, we have to work and wrestle to understand tradition. Merton argues that "convention easily becomes an evasion of reality" because we can habitually fulfil rituals that feel like sleepwalking. We're not alive to the meaning or relevance of what we're doing. We're simply doing what generations before us have done and not asking any

questions. Soon, these rituals become a dull system of ges-
tures and formalities. This is how I always saw church—sleepy
and irrelevant: people getting together, doing what they've
always done without being able to explain what it means or
why, let alone how it has changed them.

For Merton, tradition is the *opposite* of routine! He writes,
"tradition teaches us to live and shows us how to take full responsibility for our own lives." Tradition, though of course always old, is at the same time always new, because it is forever
being born again into a new generation and a new historical
context. It will be lived and applied in a new and particular
way. "Tradition nourishes the life of the spirit; convention
merely disguises its interior decay."

Tradition is therefore inherently creative! And that creative
spirit frees us to make something as ancient as pilgrimage
into a method of connecting with spaces beyond our walls,
sidewalks, and streetlights. This isn't new: philosopher and es-
sayist Henry David Thoreau, who once wrote that "every walk
is a sort of crusade," famously walked tens of miles a day to
enjoy nature and resolve writer's block. If you're worried about
distinguishing between a valid, meaningful practice and a literal walk in the park, think of what Rabbi Irwin Kula reminds
us: every tradition was once an innovation. Our souls are free
to create and invent. There are as many ways of honoring the
dead, of celebrating life, of welcoming a child into the world
as there are human beings. Just because things have been
done one way for some time does not mean they should never
evolve. What matters is whether what we're doing feels alive,

whether it is connecting us across the four levels of ourselves, one another, the natural world, and the transcendent. We have permission to create new practices, to adapt old ones, and to mix them together. And we have permission to take what we already do and affirm it as a meaningful thread of our spiritual, soulful lives.

Kursat Ozenc, cofounder of the Ritual Design Lab, offers similar advice. He explains that each of us can go ritual-spotting in our own lives to discover how we might develop a sacred practice. "Look at what's happening naturally around you. Become your own ethnographer," he says. "Maybe there's something that you enjoy doing but haven't named yet. You can amplify that by documenting all the rituals you do. It might be something from your past that you want to bring back to life, or it might be a small act that you can build on." Perhaps there's a lake, or tree, or large stone that you might walk to on the weekend, or an elderly relative you might visit and ask for family stories. Or you might try to see one new plant or animal on your morning commute every day.

On the few times that I go out for a run, I try to turn something I struggle with—exercise—into an opportunity that brings meaning and connection. If the path I'm jogging on has tree canopy above, I look up into the branches and say to the universe, "For the glory of life! I'm running for you, tree!" It sounds ridiculous, but try it! On a good day it can completely lift my spirits, and I grin from head to toe as I run. If you're worried about passersby, just look up at the sky and offer your love up to it silently. Nearly always this invokes in me a sense of awe and gratitude—and awe always locates us firmly in a place. I get to run through this world! What majesty!

CELEBRATING THE SEASONS

That connection with sky and earth, with the natural cycles of seasons, is disappearing in today's modern and increasingly urban culture. Of course, many of us still have fall potlucks with seasonal dishes. We might host summer barbeques or full moon circles that honor the time of year in their own way. On both sides of the equator, the cycle of the seasons has shaped everything from the economy to the timing of school vacations. But the reality is that many of us struggle to live in tune with the seasonal cycles, in large part because it is so easy to ignore them. We have air conditioning units and car-seat heaters, and we can buy avocados whenever we want to (for which we give thanks!). But these conveniences mean we can live our lives largely ignoring the newly flowering snow-drops or the glorious reddening leaves of Japanese maple trees. Though we may need to shovel snow or plaster on sunscreen now and then, mostly we plan work, travel, health care, and family reunions on our own timeline. It may be more conve-nient, but this way of life disconnects many of us from the natural world. Without a rhythm to our lives, we lose our spir-itual sensibility. Simply celebrating the changing weather pat-terns and seasonal celebrations is a way to bring us back into harmony with our natural landscape.

It's important to reiterate that you probably do honor the passing seasons in small and large ways already. My invitation to you is to deepen your existing practices and discover new ones to connect with the natural world. For most of us, the problem is that we are less and less engaged with nature, yet the good news is we aren't completely severed from it. Depending on where you live, honoring the seasons might involve marking the start of spring, summer, autumn, and winter or celebrating the rainy monsoon and dry seasons. From the beginning of religious culture, humans have celebrated festivals marking changes in the environment—harvest sacrifices, rain dances, and end-of-the-world solar eclipses, to name a few.

I learned to mark the seasons early. In my home village, we celebrated the feast of Michaelmas on September 29, which signified the beginning of autumn. We'd make paper lanterns, decorating the thick paper with watercolors and then attaching each lantern to a long stick. As evening came, we'd light the candle inside our lantern and walk down the street, singing. On Palm Sunday, celebrated the week before Easter, we'd bake rooster-shaped breads and attach two sticks together and decorate them with strings of fruit and candy. Off we'd march onto the golf courses of Sussex, singing. (Singing was a theme at home.) On Christmas Eve, we'd walk across muddy fields that had frozen over to gather with lanterns at the village farm's large cattle barn, where we'd be welcomed by Peter, the head farmer. Sheet music would be handed around, and for the next hour or two, we'd walk from one enclosure to another to sing Christmas carols to the various farm animals. Cows, pigs, chickens, and even the bees would be serenaded with season's greetings. After multiple verses of "O Come, O Come Emmanuel" and "Hark! The Herald Angels Sing," we'd gather in the sheep barn with mince pies and hot mulled wine to listen to Peter read the Christmas story. On Mardi Gras, we dressed up, baked pancakes (something so popular in England that we call it Pancake Day), and competed in egg-and-spoon races.

On May Day, we woke up before dawn and made our way to the heath. There, as the sun rose and we stood holding flasks of hot tea, Morris dancers emerged from the trees and started to dance to live accordion music. Bells jangled on their feet as wooden sticks clashed in complex patterns and white handkerchiefs waved to mark the arrival of spring. Later, at school, we continued celebrating May Day by braiding flower garlands and dancing around the maypole—a tradition I've kept alive to this day. While I lived in Cambridge, Massachusetts, I rose before dawn and headed to the river, where early morning revelers sang and danced around the maypole with the sun rising over the Charles River. My fellow pilgrim Caroline and I have cohosted various maypole dances, including one year when our city park party could barely withstand forty-mile-an-hour winds. The maypole itself had to be held up by volunteers while the rest of us danced merrily around it, dog walkers and parents with children joining in the fun. This past year I traveled to Washington, DC, where Caroline had set up a maypole in the middle of a quiet traffic circle! A perfect city location with plenty of curious passersby who soon were dancing with crowns made of blossoming branches.

And then in summer, as kids, we'd wait until dark on Midsummer Eve and gather to watch the largest bonfire of the year: the Saint John's Fire. In silence, we'd watch the graduating class walk toward the heap of dry wood and recite a poem in unison before lighting the enormous fire. Then they'd sing as the crowd slowly approached the flames and the fire grew smaller. After the singing, I remember watching older children compete in daring acts of jumping over the fire as it dwindled late into the night. Traditionally, the fire's ashes are spread out over farmers' fields to protect them for the coming year.

Now, during sticky summer months, Vanessa and I go night swimming. Driving to our secret swimming pond on a summer night has all the promise of renewal. Our bodies, sweaty after a long day, yearn for the cool of the water and the softness of the sand. After stripping naked, we run into the pond, shouting with delight. Then comes the rush of immersion; our bodies are home! Sometimes, we'll just lie back in silence, looking up at the stars. More often than not, I've forgotten my contact lenses and everything is a misty fog. Either way, our shoulders relax. The problems of the day seem to dissolve into the expanse of water.

REIMAGINING A LITURGICAL CALENDAR

As we excavate pieces of religious culture that have fallen away for many of us, we might think of marking celebrations as congregations do through a liturgical calendar. This calendar marks the cycles of feasts and other celebrations throughout the year, not only reminding the faithful of religious holidays but also anchoring them in a returning season. There's something wonderfully comforting about liturgical time. It doesn't travel linearly like our civic calendar, each year increasing in number. Instead, liturgical time is a never-ending circle. I love knowing that, however I succeed or fail in whatever venture or relationship, liturgical time, together with the seasons, will return again and again. This doesn't mean it's the same each time, of course, so perhaps a spiral is a better shape than just a circle. But the natural world teaches us that our own little lives take place within a celestial cadence. It helps rightsize our problems and ambitions, our losses and our longings. Estonian-born theologian Alexander Schmemann even argues that living a liturgical calendar can help us discover our power. Because liturgical time is full of feast days, living this calendar gives us natural pauses from our striving, burnout culture. "The modern world has relegated joy to the category of 'fun' and 'relaxation,'" he writes. "It is justified and permissible in our time off; it is a concession, a compromise." But, he argues, we have ceased to believe that celebration and joy have anything to do with the serious problems of the world. In fact, intentionally marking a liturgical calendar might be an answer to the very problems we face every day. For Schmemann, celebrating the seasons is a generator of power, courage, and perspective. In the face of all our contemporary woes, celebrating these seasonal moments is a generator of joy.

Of course, the festivals I grew up with come from northern Europe and signify elements of the Christian story. But you can draw on your own ancestry and cultural roots. Whatever you believe, these practices become magical in our memory. The beauty, the transformed landscapes, the laughter—each one a comfort in the mind's eye. Knowing that these festivals return every year offers solidity and welcome as the year progresses. Benedictine nun Joan Chittister refers to the repeating liturgical calendar as "an exercise in spiritual ripening." Though the festivals don't change, we do. Our lives are leavened with the yeast of celebration. The year comes alive to our imagination—meaning there's always something to look forward to.

Spend some time reflecting on what festivals you might want to celebrate, or how the ones you already do can be deepened so they are meaningful bridges of connection with nature. Maybe these festivals mark moments you shared with your family—Eid al-Fitr, Día de los Muertos, Christmas, Juneteenth, or Rosh Hashanah. Perhaps you draw on civic or sporting celebrations, or something from the movies—Groundhog Day, Valentine's Day, baseball's opening day. Or maybe you make a point to have a party at the beginning of each season—spring, summer, autumn, and winter—and you can choose whether to be explicit about it, with activities and decorations, or keep the reason for your quarterly parties a liturgical secret.

I know that I need to celebrate especially when times are tough. February is hard enough as it is, but in Boston, the earliest signs of spring don't come until late March, so late winter is my least favorite time of year. Since marrying Sean, I have delighted, therefore, that March is also the year's pinnacle for college basketball. Cheering for the Kentucky Wildcats, while trying to figure out some of the rules of basketball, has become an annual tradition. Even though I don't follow the team through the rest of the year and don't have much in common culturally with my parents-in-law, who are die-hard members of the Big Blue Nation, this is a moment where I join long text threads to share the moments of basketball-themed excitement and inevitable heartbreak together. The NCAA March Madness tournament has become, for me, the signal that winter will soon be over and everything will be okay.

In addition to ringing in seasons or revering certain holidays that mark a new cycle of the year, think about how you might integrate nature into other celebrations. When celebrating the British leg of our wedding, my parents asked all our guests to bring hiking boots or sensible walking shoes. Since the party was in August, we wanted to make the time of year a part of the festivities. Before cake was served, we headed for a long walk into the woodlands behind my parents' home. Just like sitting around the dinner table, a shared walk allows people to talk easily, without pressure. You can drift from one conversation to another, or simply take some time on your own. The landscape you walk through will bring your celebration to life.

There is much to mine from ancient traditions to create modern seasonal celebrations, but there are also contemporary communities and rituals that are already doing this work.

A growing number of women's, men's, and LGBTQ+ groups gather around the lunar calendar, bringing a regular rhythm to getting together and sharing space for intimacy and connection. Drawing on tradition, one of these groups—At the Well—connects women to body, soul, and community through wellness education and Jewish spirituality. Sarah Waxman and her team are reviving the Hebrew calendar in all its cyclical, lunar glory to celebrate a new iteration of Rosh Chodesh—the first day after a new moon. Gathering every month, Well Circles around the country give women space to connect, learn, and be heard. Each month the community creates a new Moon Manual for the circles to use, filled with inspiring stories, creative exercises, recipes, and poems—all collected from female leaders around the world.

Other communities, like the Artisan's Asylum in Somerville, Massachusetts, adapt traditional annual festivals to create their own community calendar. Each year, the jewelry makers, 3-D print artists, woodworkers, and other artists who use the maker space get together to celebrate Makersgiving during the Thanksgiving season. Not only do they each contribute a potluck dish, but they offer something they have made in the shared workshop space during the year and add it to the table, creating a veritable feast of creativity. The fall season takes on a new significance for these artists: it is a time to show and celebrate their work from the past year.

Of course, the power in these celebrations is not just doing it once. The wisdom of marking the seasons is that we return to them year in and year out. In doing so, we notice things in nature that we may not have noticed before. We may keep an eye out for certain spring flowers to let us know that May Day is approaching. We might notice that the sun is lower in the sky than it was the prior week, reminding us that the fall equinox is coming. Smells of decaying leaves or freshly cut grass, the sight of longer shadows or baby deer, and the sound of a goldfinch or overflowing creek all tell us where we are in nature's cycle. You probably have your own signs that you notice. The celebrations we keep each year remind us to pay attention and keep seasonal time. You know when the tradition has seeped deep into you when your children, friends, or family start to mark the moment even when you're not there. For example, when I was growing up I went to hear Bach's *Saint Matthew Passion* every Good Friday, and even though I now live far away from my family, I'll make sure I listen to the three-hour epic piece of classical music all the way through at least once before Easter. It just wouldn't feel right if I didn't.

CELEBRATING NATURE WHEN YOU LIVE IN THE CITY

Connecting with nature is, of the four connections, the most challenging for me. I live in a city, where it takes real effort to take myself out of the built environment. The hordes of tourists who walk underneath my window each morning make it difficult to concentrate on the soft light of the morning sun. Nonetheless, if we're intentional, to return to natural beauty doesn't demand distant travel or breathtaking vistas. For example, there's a single tree that stands outside my window in the middle of Harvard Yard. It is an unremarkable tree—neither the tallest nor the fullest. But I've come to think of this tree as a testament to beauty and wildness in the midst of the cement and built structures of the city. Each morning as I sit on my meditation cushion, I spend the last minute or so just gazing at the tree. I have fallen a little bit in love with this tree—so much so that I think of it even when I travel, meditating in a hotel room or when staying with friends. Paying attention to it every morning, I notice the subtle signs of passing time. Just like celebrating the seasons, simply noticing this tree every day gives me a rhythm.

When we do look out onto nature, so much depends on how we see. Do we see a location (dead space) or a living universe (a landscape alive with possibility)? The outer world becomes a metaphor for our own, unknown, inner landscape. Sometimes the bare tree in the drab, gray morning rain speaks to my sadness in a way I hadn't yet found words for. Or my eye will catch a bird in its branches, flying back and forth, mirroring how my own brain travels back and forth, back and forth. In this way, we can look out at the natural world as if it were a sacred text, "rereading" the view from one window again and again to find new connections, new meaning. You can try this by buying plants to keep indoors or on your stoop and focusing your gaze on the veins of a single leaf. Paternity cofounder Anna Murray calls this "musing on the micro." Or you can muse on the macro by finding a spot from where you can watch the sky change from day to dusk to return to the earth's natural rhythm.

John O'Donohue writes that paying attention to beauty in the world cultivates the sacred within us. "Beauty addresses us from a place beyond; it captures our complete attention because it resonates with the sense of the beyond that is already in us; in this sense beauty is the ideal visitation; it settles at once into that 'elsewhere' within us." Think of Anne Frank looking out onto a small courtyard from the secret annex in which she was hidden. For two years she looked at the same small square of sky, birds, and chestnut tree and was somehow able to conjure a magnificent inner life as the claws of Nazi occupation and the betrayal of neighbors came ever closer.

It may be that this discipline to notice nature amid the constraints of concrete helps us develop a keener eye. In middle school biology class, I was given a one-meter wire square and had to count how many plant species I could find within it. Each blade of grass suddenly took on momentous importance. A new world opened up: daisies, dandelions, garlic mustard, a stray thistle. Even a ladybug and a crane fly. This is what it takes to learn how to pay attention to nature when you don't have a single tree on your block to tell you whether spring is coming. Revel in the evidence of the seasons that you do see. On a simple lawn, as the eighteenth-century rabbi Nachman of Breslov would say, even the grass can awaken our hearts.

Even if we can't leave the house, nature can come to us. With each passing season my mother decorated a small table in our house's entryway. It featured books or a painting reflecting the time of year, like mushrooms, say, in early autumn. Or it would have tall branches in springtime with home-decorated Easter eggs. Large pumpkins around Halloween. An enormous wreath of evergreens and holly in December. Today, rather than a nature table my husband arranges flowers and greens: pink ranunculus, white peonies, tall grasses, sweet peas. They too announce the passing rhythm of the seasons. I've found that a simple handpicked bouquet can infuse us with what the Scottish writer Richard Holloway describes as "the sense many of us can't quite shake off, that though it does not explain itself, nevertheless the universe seems to have known we were coming." That somehow we belong to the universe, that witnessing nature's beauty is a homecoming, bringing a sense of completion and sureness to our lives.

WORLD AS LOVER, WORLD AS SELF

One day, when I was eight or nine years old, I walked home from school to find twelve adults pretending to be carrots in our back garden. They started off crouching on the ground, as small as they could make themselves, and gradually stretched out to stand tall, on tiptoes. Leading them was a Hungarian-Israeli friend of my mother's, Jutka Harstein. She wanted to teach cooking classes, so my mother offered her our kitchen. A dozen people gathered there to learn how to make goulash and the perfect veggie burgers. (Our family still talks about them twenty-five years later.) Jutka's genius was that she never wasted anything. Vegetable skins became tomorrow's soup stock or a refreshing smoothie. To teach this mind-set, she didn't start her cooking classes by explaining knives and heating temperatures—but instead invited everyone to embody the food itself. Each student had to embody a carrot's life cycle in order to fully grasp the nutritious gifts it had to offer. Hence the group exercise in our garden!

What this practice reveals is a core paradigm shift that can be difficult to grasp in the twenty-first century. So far, we've looked at practices that help us connect from our human bodies to the natural world. But this final practice asks something different. Instead of seeing ourselves as separate from our landscapes, we can understand ourselves to be the landscape itself.

Joanna Macy, the great Buddhist environmental activist, explains that "the world itself, if we are bold to love it, acts through us. It does not ask us to be pure or perfect, or wait until we are detached from all passions, but only to care, to harness the sweet, pure intention of our deepest passions." She introduces four worldviews through which we understand our relationship to the natural world, two of which dominate our thinking today and two that might totally transform how we understand ourselves and shift our destructive species behavior.

The first is to think of the world as a battlefield in which the forces of good fight the forces of evil. In this frame of mind, the earth is a resource to be mined and shaped to meet our human desires. The natural landscape is a backdrop for our human drama, and any damage done is an unfortunate externality to our greater purpose. Think of what you see in newspaper headlines or listen to the way that most business leaders and policy makers talk. In this paradigm, preserving "the environment" clashes with goals to grow the economy, so strip-mining, drilling, and dumping waste are an unfortunate necessity. Our own smaller-scale version of this frame is to see our own lives as distinct from the natural world. We might visit natural vistas or landscapes during a vacation, for example, but by and large nature is "out there" and far away from us.

Macy identifies the second paradigm as viewing the world as a trap. Here, any attachment to physical reality is an impediment to our great spiritual journey. Think of self-consciously spiritual people who dismiss earthly realities because they're focused purely on a "higher consciousness." This frame follows a simplistic reading of the Platonic tradition in which the most real thing is the nonphysical realm. The earth is simply beautiful background scenery to our individual enlightenment. This makes little sense on closer inspection, even within Buddhist metaphysics. The Buddha taught detachment from ego, not detachment from the world. "Trying to escape from something that we are dependent on breeds a love-hate relationship with it. [This] inflames a two-fold desire—to destroy and to possess," explains Macy in her book *World as Lover, World as Self.*

These two ways of thinking shape much of our reality. To try to protect rainforests and rivers from industrial use, environmental campaigners have to demonstrate the economic value of these "assets" so they will be deemed valuable for our growth-obsessed economic system. When we see nature's purpose as serving our needs—or as an impediment to our success we condemn it to destruction. We focus on our own individual spiritual growth without understanding the interconnectedness of all things.

Instead, argues Macy, we might think of the world as our lover. "When you see the world as lover, every being, every phenomenon, can become . . . an expression of that ongoing, erotic impulse." The wind rustling through the trees whispers our name. The lapping waves caress our skin. That pilgrim's tea is a love letter from the earth. It can be a challenging reframe. Like a partner who has been away too long from their spouse, it can feel overly intimate, confrontational even. This way of thinking challenges us to be present in nature much more often because we'll learn to fall in love with it again.

In 2008 I was outrageously lucky to be one of twenty young people to join a ten-day voyage to the Arctic with the World Wildlife Fund to learn about the impacts of melting arctic sea ice. I'd heard about the high north, of course, and vaguely understood how losing ice mass would cause rising seas around the world. After lectures from scientists and site visits to understand the changes firsthand, what really anchored my perspective was seeing a polar bear playing in the snow. Standing on the boat deck in a T-shirt as the too-warm sun shone down on us, I fell completely in love with the Arctic, from the little purple flowers to the enormous ice glaciers. I came back armed not only with a solid understanding of climate science but with an intrinsic love for this precious landscape, which is on track to completely disappear in a few decades. You might also think of how Native American and First Nation peoples at Standing Rock called themselves "protectors," not "protestors," as they temporarily stopped the Dakota Access Pipeline being built through their land. They were protecting the inherent value of it.

In Australia and Canada, it is common for public events to start with an acknowledgment that a gathering is taking place on Native land. The United States has a long and painful history of land seizures that not only robbed Native peoples of land and free movement but also destroyed spiritually rich connections to place and identity. The US Department of Arts and Culture, a grassroots action network, has a beautiful tool kit for honoring Native land at gatherings—town halls, business conferences, even weddings—and in my experience of practicing honoring Native land at the opening of our How We Gather convenings, it changes the ways in which all of us relate to the place we are visiting. Taking a moment to witness the place and the people who have lived in it infuses an event with deeper significance and a larger context. Of course, religious and cultural traditions have long revered natural places. Shinto shrines flank the base of Fuji-san (Mount Fuji); the Chaga people of Tanzania revere Mount Kilimanjaro; while the ancient Greeks had Mount Olympus.

More recently, millions of people have fallen in love with the natural world by watching the BBC's television series *Planet Earth* and *Blue Planet*. The incredible camera shots bring to life hidden corners of the world as more than mere articles of interest; the plants and animals stir our hearts in love and protection. When watching a show that awakens this kind of reverence and connection, try to hold on to it by journaling or simply breathing consciously to remember that sense of deep comfort. Or if you have a pet, try expanding the love you have for your dog or cat or other animal to all animals and living things.

The fourth and final paradigm Macy invites us into is seeing the world as self. No longer is nature something outside of us, a landscape for us to admire or even to love—instead, we *are* nature. We are the world itself. The great environmental activist John Seed embodies this when he says, "I try to remember that it's not me, John, trying to protect the rainforest. Rather, I am part of the rainforest protecting itself. I am that part of the rainforest recently emerged into human thinking." It is destabilizing to think this way, but my sense is that we've each had moments of this kind of experience: the flash of mysterious at-home-ness when we look at a night sky, the magical feeling of being both an inconsequent speck amid a vast landscape and yet as uncountably large as the universe itself. That both/and world is where Macy wants us to live. In this shift of identity, we move from an isolated "I" to "a vaster sense of what we are." This paradigm is known as deep ecology, and it's the very thing Jutka was teaching by making her cooking students pretend they were carrots. Physically embodying the natural world helps shift our mindset to remind us, in some greater cosmic wisdom, that we *are* the carrot!

I know that if I am not careful, I bottle away the sadness I feel when reading about the BP oil spill or the starvation of wild polar bears or the extreme species loss we're experiencing. After only three years of full-time activism mobilizing young people around the United Nations climate change targets, the pain was overwhelming, and I burned out. I felt stupid for getting so emotionally involved, but how can we avoid it? As we enter a deeper consciousness of the natural world, I find some small amount of comfort knowing that even as weather patterns change frantically and we'll enter a long period of water stress, food crisis, and climate refugees, the earth itself will stabilize as the millennia pass. Sadly, whether humans survive as a species is a different question altogether.

Our dominant culture has little place for this environmental anxiety and grief, and we learn to shut down that inherent empathy and to separate ourselves from our surroundings. In his essay "Ecology and Man," environmentalist Paul Shepard explains that this is counter to our innate biology. "Our thought forms, our language, encourage us to see ourselves or a plant or an animal as an isolated sac, a thing, a contained self, whereas the epidermis of the skin is ecologically like a pond surface or a forest soil, not a shell so much as a delicate interpenetration." The boundaries we've been taught to see are actually gateways of connection. A simple practice to reconnect with this perspective is to verbalize the landscape you are in as if you are the landscape speaking, just like John Seed models: "I am the pond, and the pond is me" or "The wind moving through my branches feels chilly."

Being at Home in the World

I have no doubt that you already have your own ways of connecting to nature and that these practices can deeply enrich your spiritual life. Perhaps you'll focus on honoring the elements—air, earth, water, fire—out in the world by going cliff diving or sitting around a bonfire. Or you'll create spaces to honor the elements at home: lighting a candle, having a bath, practicing conscious breathing, tending a potted plant. You might celebrate Chinese New Year or the Japanese festival of Tanabata, weaving written wishes into colorful strips of paper and hanging them from bamboo or trees. You might go for a Christmas Day walk or immerse in water on the day before Yom Kippur. You might visit a certain tree when you walk the dog or go for a run. You might start gardening or arranging flowers. Perhaps you'll create your own nature table or an altar with your favorite shells, feathers, stones, and pressed flowers. Whatever practices you already have or want to explore, draw on the context of your landscape to inspire you.

You can also reflect on your own natural holy places. Where do you come from? Where does your family's history lie? What places have defined you? You might take on a healing journey or simply start to take a long walk once a week. You can make a pilgrimage anytime, anywhere, along a Great Route or from your back door out into the world. Maybe your place of pilgrimage is your grandparents' backyard, the ocean, an orchard, or a little park in the midst of the city. Or you might turn a trip to visit someone you love into a pilgrimage. As my pilgrim guide Will Parsons says, "Our spiritual landscape is open to all."

You might also simply stay where you are, find a place on the earth, and look up at the sky, knowing that here you are home.

CHAPTER 4

Connecting with Transcendence

M Y FIRST REAL JOB was washing dishes at the local village pub. Each weekend shift earned me enough money to buy a new Agatha Christie murder mystery, some gel pens (ideally scented), a magazine, and copious amounts of chocolate. On my weekly mini shopping spree, I'd pass supermarkets, an upmarket sound system supplier, and my favorite store—Between the Lines. To my thirteen-year-old self, this store represented everything that an adult life of leisure had to offer. Things that were nice but not necessary: wicker baskets, candles, Danish-designed cushions, and, best of all, a wide selection of spa music and essential oils.

It took me a year before I was brave enough to go inside. Even then, I walked past the display windows three times before I went in. I'd seen commercials for spa resorts on TV, and thinking this the ultimate haven of peace and safety to contrast against the cluster of hormones that was my boys' boarding house, I wanted to recreate this bathrobe-clad scene in my own bedroom. I bought a CD of ocean waves overlaying Pachelbel's Canon and some lavender-scented essential oil, without being clear how exactly to use it but confident in my ability to find a way.

Once home, I put on the music, with seascape sounds and all, and rubbed the oil into the palms of my hands. I made sure I was all alone and closed my eyes. Standing, bare-chested, I moved my hands just above the surface of my body, massaging the air almost, and then placed my hands over my heart. Tears welled up, and then I could no longer hold them back. I cried. For a long time. Not because I was particularly sad in that moment, but because the "I" that felt sadness had melted into something much bigger than myself that could hold all the enormity of the pain and sadness that is in any human life. The sounds of the ocean and the smell of the lavender suggested a larger presence, which was both me and not me, and it didn't flinch from my tears. Without being able to explain why, I felt like the universe knew the depth of my suffering and that somehow everything would be okay.

So many of us have stories like this. We have moments in which we feel a bridge has appeared between us and something beyond. That bridge can come along when we explore a homemade ritual that we, now and then, revisit but never talk about. Those moments feel mysterious because we can't rationalize what's happened. Though they feel special, sacred even, afterward we feel embarrassed and uncomfortable. "What the hell was I doing? I don't even believe in that stuff! Massaging my aura?! Let's never tell anyone about that. Ever." It can be disconcerting. We're not in control when we give ourselves over to an experience like this. We've handed over our power, we've fully let go, and later we come back to ourselves with what Brené Brown calls a vulnerability hangover.

I've learned to understand moments like this as prayer. I've always been suspicious of that word, but I've discovered that prayer practices are beautiful, powerful, and perhaps even necessary for us to feel deeply connected to what is beyond us.

Prayer Isn't What We Think It Is

I had always thought of prayer as the most ridiculous element of religion. It seemed absurd to go to a magical vending machine in the sky and ask god for the things you wanted. I'd heard stories of people not taking their lifesaving medicine because they would be "healed by prayer," and I'd read about parents telling their children to "pray the gay away." Prayer wasn't just ridiculous—it seemed actively harmful. It belonged to a time when we didn't understand how diseases spread or how weather patterns changed. Prayer was, in short, for fools.

But today, I understand it differently. It still isn't a heavenly jukebox. It isn't, at its heart, about just asking for what you want. And it definitely isn't confined to words said while kneeling at our bedside, palms touching and head bowed. Instead, the practice of prayer is about being conscious of—and telling the truth about—how we really feel and think, taking what has been unconscious and bringing it into open awareness. Scholar of psychiatry and religion Ann Ulanov and jazz critic Barry Ulanov call this kind of prayer "primary speech." "Everybody prays," they write. "To pray is to listen to and hear this self who is speaking. . . . In prayer we say who in fact we are." Prayer is about listening to what our hearts know to be true: the deep loves and longings that live within everyone.

The great Russian Orthodox writer Anthony Bloom talks about true prayer being the process through which things "suddenly disclose themselves with a depth we have never before perceived or when we suddenly discover in ourselves a depth." This experience is wonderfully, and sometimes frighteningly, freeing. It gives us "the sense that we are free from possession, and this freedom establishes us in a relationship where everything is love—human love and love divine." Bloom knew of which he spoke. Growing up in Iran and Russia, he served as a surgeon on the front lines with the French Army in the Second World War.

Prayer is the path toward ever greater love. It fuses our human love with what Bloom calls "divine love," but you can translate that to whatever language opens your heart. For me, it's that sense of something more, something greater than myself that is fundamentally mysterious and forever beyond language. To practice prayer is to continually return to this path of love. Because our lives are so full, Bloom writes in his book *Beginning to Pray*, "we may imagine that there can be nothing more than this, that we have found fulfillment and wholeness, that we have reached the end of our search. But we must learn that there is always more."

So how do we practice prayer? Chances are, you're already doing it. In this chapter, we'll look at four types of prayer: adoration, contrition, thanksgiving, and supplication. I've chosen these old-fashioned words because it feels good to know that we're following the well-trodden path of generations before us. That isn't to say we should feel the need to legitimize our modern practices with ancient and archaic definitions; it simply means this is another case of recovering valuable wisdom from the treasures locked up inside religious traditions. My friend Sister of Saint Joseph Carol Zinn, a smart, powerful, hilarious woman who has lived for many years as a Catholic nun, taught me this four-part prayer practice, and it has become the foundation of my mornings ever since. You can follow these four stages in the shower, on the bus, on a meditation cushion, or before you fall asleep. You can write words in a journal or make art with a friend; you can do it inside or outside, in five minutes or five hours—there are a million ways to give shape to a prayer practice. What I hope to share is a framework that you can map onto what you're already doing to help ground and deepen it, to find a deeper connection to that something that is greater than all of us.

ADORATION

Ironically, the first step to deeper awareness isn't about introspection. It's about getting radically *away* from ourselves, to decenter our individual experience and seek to place ourselves in service of, or to become part of, something bigger than us. If the first level of connection that we explored in Chapter 1 is about connecting deeply to yourself, this practice is about connecting to a great otherness.

You might have experienced this sense of collective union at a music festival, on the streets at a protest, or in the middle of a sports arena. Perhaps you've tried a retreat experience which has reset your perspective, or you have a mindfulness or meditation practice. Even the smallest spaces can help us connect with something greater. Before moving into our own apartment, Sean and I lived with three wonderful housemates, meaning that the only spot in our apartment where I could be assured to be alone was our dusty winter coat closet. There, amid the piles of toolboxes and snow boots, I stored my meditation cushion. For the two years we lived on Trowbridge Street, I'd climb into the closet first thing in the morning and start my meditation time by listening to a piece of music. Sixteenth-century motets like "Ego flos campi" by Jacob Clemens non Papa and contemporary compositions like Arvo Pärt's haunting "Spiegel im Spiegel" brought me into a prayerful time. Both pieces have an ethereal quality that helps me connect with that "something more" and feel calm. Though I had dismissed prayer's power to heal others, there's growing evidence that taking this kind of intentional time has numerous health benefits for ourselves. Cardiologist and professor at Harvard Medical School, and a pioneer in the field of mind/body medicine, Dr. Herbert Benson discovered what he calls "the relaxation response," which occurs during periods of prayer and meditation. At such times, the body's metabolism decreases, the heart rate slows, blood pressure goes down, and our breath becomes more relaxed and regular.

Traditionally, of course, adoration would have been about explicitly worshipping god. This might resonate for some, but if it doesn't, I suggest that you find ways of lifting your attention toward the larger beauty of the world, to the greater connection that holds all things. You might want to read a poem to yourself or find a small selection of music tracks that move you. And of course, if god language works for you—go for it! What matters to me is that sense of adoration of something bigger than ourselves. Theologian Renita J. Weems argues that we are wired for worship, so we are going to end up worshipping something. Better to be intentional about what that something is instead of falling into the trap of worshipping money, status, and power—as so much of our dominant culture does.

One of my favorite ways of decentering is to get a good massage! This is a luxury, but its value is enormous. Of course, having someone give you a back rub feels relaxing, but I've realized that there's more beyond that. I have some of my most creative insights about myself, my relationships, and my work while I'm being stretched and kneaded on the massage table.

It's where I've been hit with profound but difficult insights about needing to apologize to someone, deciding to leave a job, or creating boundaries in a destructive relationship. In the hands of my amazing masseuse Misty, I am fully present to my body for a rare spell of time. As she squeezes and molds, I try to imagine that her hands are ambassadors of the eternal as she works divine care and strength into my body.

A growing trend today is the exploration of psychedelics, especially ayahuasca, to help people connect to a sense of the divine. Though some people experience powerful ceremonies, especially when the drug experience is facilitated by a wisdom teacher or guide, I remain hesitant about the use of psychedel-ics as a lone spiritual practice, mostly because, to paraphrase religious scholar Huston Smith, a spiritual experience does not by itself make a spiritual life. In his book *How to Change Your Mind*, Michael Pollan explains, "Integration is essential to making sense of the experience, whether in or out of the med-ical context. Or else it remains just a drug experience." I'm also wary of spiritual tourism in which we desperately seek out transformative experiences that come from cultures that are not our own. We run the risk of picking only the exciting el-ements of these traditions without understanding the deeper significance and context—a particular danger with traditions that have been marginalized and colonized, such as indige-nous practices. We also miss out on the chance to learn more about the hidden gems of our own backgrounds and cultures! Therefore, instead of looking to hallucinogenic substances, I suggest we draw on simple tools for cultivating attention so that we can more consistently reorient ourselves toward the elements of life that are greater than ourselves.

Cultivating attention is so powerful that French activist and mystic Simone Weil famously argued that even concentrating on a difficult math problem prepared oneself for prayer. In *Waiting for God*, she explains that "if we concentrate our attention on trying to solve a problem of geometry, and if at the end of an hour we are no nearer to doing so than at the beginning, we have nevertheless been making progress each minute of that hour in another more mysterious dimension." Despite it feeling like nothing is happening, Weil promises us that our apparently barren efforts nonetheless lead to bringing more light into the soul—even without feeling or knowing it.

Weil knew about forging her own spiritual path because she was an outsider. Growing up in France, among a mostly agnostic, secular Jewish family, she suffered multiple health challenges throughout her childhood and later life. Living through the First World War, she went on to study alongside Simone de Beauvoir and was known for her radical political views. She joined the French General Strike of 1933, and her involvement in workers' rights fundamentally shaped her spirituality of solidarity. As she grew older, her mystical sensibility was cultivated by her friendship with a Catholic priest and led her deeper into a religious life—but one always outside of institutions. She refused to be baptized and would only witness, rather than take part in, the celebration of the Eucharist. For Weil, the key to spiritual practice was "the realization that prayer consists of attention. It is the orientation of all the attention of which the soul is capable toward God. The quality of the attention counts for much in the quality of the prayer."

Of course, cultivating prayerful attention and awareness doesn't just happen through geometry studies! One of the communities from which I learned the most about prayer during our *How We Gather* research was the Sanctuaries in Washington, DC. Here, artists collaborated across disciplines to create experiences and expressions of their spirituality in service of social justice and healing. Sanctuaries' artists have helped to secure legal representation for refugees through screenprinting, prevented the displacement of public housing residents through hip-hop, and mobilized thousands of people to advocate for environmental justice, racial equity, and the dignity of the poor through the visual and performing arts. Made of people with wildly different religious and racial identities, and always moving across the city in order to not become pigeonholed as belonging to one corner of town, they bring together unlikely collaborations, like a classical Indian musician collaborating with a hip-hop artist, a jewelry workshop inspired by Jewish text, and spoken word melded with live painting at a Soul Slam.

Set up in 2013 by a team led by Erik Martínez Resly, or simply Rev. Erik as he's known to the community, the Sanctuaries always wove spirituality, social justice, and the creative arts together. "We already have language in the arts that speak to the life of the soul: find your flow, get in the groove, be in the zone. There's a sense that my body is caught up in a movement that is larger than myself. I have surrendered to a power, a force, a source of inspiration that I can touch or tap into, but that I can never fully control. It's not mine alone. That's the starting point for us. We've found that some of the best practices in justice-making overlap with some of the best practices in making art and deepening our spiritual lives," explains Rev. Erik.

What the Sanctuaries teaches us is that prayer can be movement, it can be art, and it can be creative. "We're not introducing something new. But in the midst of a society that is speeding up and increasingly selling us on the illusion of control, we're taking a moment to slow down and notice that which cannot be done in an individualistic way." The leaders of the Sanctuaries, whether they stitch, sing, rap, or dance, are creating entrances into a deeper experience of the world. Over and over again, explains Erik, it is in the creative flow that people enter that the artists say they connect with the fullness of the world. "People tend to speak about their experience in a beautifully mysterious way: the very same moment when they feel connected to something more than themselves is when they also feel most authentically true to themselves. 'I didn't come up with this poem, it came to me from somewhere else, but it's who I really am most deeply.' It's a paradox! We are our truest selves and totally not ourselves at the very same time."

CONTRITION

The second type of prayer is contrition. Here we bring to awareness the ways in which we have fallen short of how we

want to be and behave in the world. We ask ourselves questions like, What have I done that has caused pain or suffering?
What have I left undone that might have served others? For
what do I need forgiveness?

It's very likely that you already do a form of this regularly,
either when you forget a birthday or lie awake obsessing over
something you said that day. Some days a list of complete
failures rolls off my tongue—letting down a friend at the last
minute, ignoring the needs of someone on the street, being
too afraid to speak up in a situation when I know I should
have—and on others I can barely think of more than one fail-
ure. (Clearly this has nothing to do with my actual actions,
but more my ability to tune in to the truth!) Unsurprisingly,
contrition can be the least pleasant part of prayer time. I haven't yet met anyone who likes being confronted with their
shortcomings. But it isn't about being berated or shamed by
an inner judgmental voice. It is the recognition that we all
have sufficient insufficiencies. Think of it as a chance to
adjust your sails while speeding across the water. Realizing
we're off track and making changes now, as best we can, will
save us enormous efforts later on when we've gone much further across the sea. On some days, when I sit down on my
meditation cushion feeling stridently righteous and angry, I
find that when I listen to this inner knowing I'm confronted
with the fact that I made just as many mistakes as anyone
else. Prayer is not always satisfying. Often the most valuable
moments of prayer are when our preset assumptions are un-
raveled and a new insight emerges, though this can take time.

Scholar Mark Jordan reminds us that what is most important isn't how we feel during prayer time, but what happens afterward.

But this prayer of contrition can also be enormously refreshing. Finally! A chance to be honest, witnessed by the great beyond, about what's going on and confront the way we want to show up in the world: braver and free.

But how do we ensure we don't get stuck in cycles of shame and overwhelm? By moving our bodies together with the words we say out loud. At our How We Gather convenings, where we brought together innovative community leaders from across the country, we invited participants to lead one another in practices that belonged to their community. At one such session, Edina Lekovic, former director of community outreach for the Women's Mosque of America in Los Angeles, led us in a cycle of Muslim prayer. As most of us were unfamiliar with Arabic, Edina had printed out a translation, and we were able to echo her Arabic with our English. The call-and-response was evocative, but what struck me most was the power of movement in prayer. Standing, kneeling, leaning forward to place our foreheads on the carpet. Back up again and down again, hands next to our faces. This shouldn't have been surprising! Before it became the norm to clasp hands together in prayer, Christians stood in prayer, with their elbows close to the sides of their bodies and with hands outstretched sideways, palms up. Jews customarily take three steps back and three steps forward when beginning the Amidah, the core of every worship service. Many prayer traditions include bowing or swaying or dancing. The Zohar, a mystical Jewish text, teaches that when we utter sacred words of prayer, the light in our soul is kindled, and we sway to and fro like the flame of a candle.

So as you take time for contrition, explore how you might incorporate physical movement. My experience has been that on the days where there is simply too much to say, sitting on my knees and bowing forward, placing my head on the floor, offers its own prayer of contrition. If you've never tried it before—have a go. It is wonderfully liberating.

Perhaps my favorite form of contrition is not reflecting alone, but together. Joining—or starting—a small group is one of the most powerful spiritual practices we can commit to, because a good small group is loving enough for us to be supported and held, but accountable enough to not let us get away with platitudes and easy answers. You might recognize this as a covenant group, a regular gathering of a small number of people from the same congregation, perhaps three to six or so, who get together to share what is really going on in their lives. It isn't just a collection of friends who get together, but rather a committed group of trusted people who travel through life with you. The same goes for whatever kind of secular small group you create: a book group, for instance, that talks about the book but really talks about life's difficult questions. As you share your shortcomings in a safe way, you'll find that these people will love you and hold you responsible for your actions. They don't need to believe in the same things you do, nor use the same language to describe their spiritual practices. Nor do they even need to be your closest friends. But they will start to matter enormously.

I have been a member of several small groups, and in my longest-running group, I got together every month with a Buddhist, an Episcopalian, a Catholic, and a None-of-the-Above. When we started, most of us only knew one another vaguely. All of us were looking to deepen our commitment to the spiritual element of our lives, and all of us felt stuck in the traditional communities of which we were a part, if any. We needed a place where we could speak frankly and safely about what was really going on in our lives. This is a particular relief when you are responsible for others and have to be the "responsible adult" in most groups you're in.

Our practice was simple. Every month, we got together in one of our apartments, ordered in Thai food (rituals can be delicious!), and spent time sharing the state of our souls. We called it, at first jokingly, our Confession Group because this was the intimate community with whom we felt totally safe to take off the masks of success and okayness and be brutally honest. One by one, each of us would spend ten to fifteen minutes sharing some aspect of our life in which we were struggling: finances, romantic partnership, resentment, relationship with parents, ambition, our body, grief. By now, we're aware of the power of vulnerability, but so rarely do we have a place where we can tell the ugliest truths about ourselves and know that we will still be fiercely loved. After sharing (and we'd use a timer to keep us on track), the other group members offered questions, reflected back patterns that they noticed, or—when invited—offered advice based on their own experience.

Practicing contrition in a small group breaks down the common assumption, when we're on our own or in large groups, that our problems are much worse or more shameful or more unusual than everybody else's. The unexpected joy of a small group of love and accountability is that we learn that others have problems just as we do and that the list of issues where we feel like failures is often not that different from everyone else. Even in the moments where I was challenged to see something from a different perspective or was held accountable to the values I had said were important to me, I always left the gathering grateful, renewed, and invigorated. Of any similar experience, the closest I can compare it to is coming out as gay as a teenager. The heaviness of pain and sadness that I had lived with for sixteen years suddenly started to fall away. In my society-induced secretiveness, the shame had buried itself in how I dressed, walked, spoke, and who I chose to spend time with. It made me afraid to be honest, because I desperately didn't want to be found out. Then as I started to tell trustworthy people, suddenly this secret lost its power over me, and I was able to reconnect to parts of myself that I had had to disconnect from. A safe and loving confession group feels like that too. I would often forget how much I'd needed small group time until after we'd finished.

Creating a small group is easier than you might think. I've seen versions of these honest conversations happen among friends who gather every Sunday night to talk about baseball and who take a preseason weekend away each year to dig deep together, and among a group of moms who meet every month for breakfast. It usually helps to gather with people who are slightly adjacent to your everyday life rather than deeply connected to it. That's why doing this with strangers at first can be so effective! Secular congregations like Sunday Assembly have created "smoups" (their humorously named small groups), and leadership trainings often employ the use of small groups too. Think of personal-growth programs like the Landmark Forum or Harvard Business School professor Bill George's True North small groups, where people can gather to have in-depth discussions and share intimately about the most important things in their lives. The ultimate example of confessional small groups remains recovery communities like Alcoholics Anonymous, where anyone is able to join a group and share, safely and in confidence, how they're struggling or making progress in their sobriety journey.

The gift we can offer one another is our loving, listening presence. A group flourishes when it is neither invasive nor evasive. It walks the delicate line of support and accountability, which John Wesley, founder of the Methodist movement, famously described as "watching over one another in love." It helps us live our lives with integrity. Journeying with others in the same general direction means we don't lose sight of our values, the things we know matter but sometimes might fade away among the shiny lights of achievement or the sinkholes of despair. In our low moments, small groups can lift us up again. If these people, who know all our inner ugliness and still love us, believe that we can change the situation and trust in our willingness to try, then perhaps we can do more, be more, than we expect of ourselves. Ideally, the groups are small in size and high in commitment. You have to be able to rely on one another. In my own group, we committed each year to continue for twelve months, giving us a way out if, after some time, we needed to reassess what we were able to give. The result is not only a better understanding of ourselves, but a better sense of what is beyond ourselves. Contrition is about looking inward, yes, but it's also about seeing how we impact the larger picture of the universe.

THANKSGIVING

After the introspection of contrition comes thanksgiving, in which we list the people and things for which we are grateful. In my own practice, I'll often start with the fact that I'm alive. I'll remember the kindnesses shown to me over the last day. The chances to learn and to be of service. My body. Specific people who bring meaning and joy. One of my favorite ways to offer thanks is to make a gratitude chain, linking one thing to another. For example, to be grateful for yesterday's dinner with friends links to the beauty of the tableware, which reminds me of my family's celebration at our dining table, which reminds me of my grandmother's artistry—all of which I am grateful for. One *Harry Potter and the Sacred Text* listener told us that she starts her chain of gratitude by saying, "I'm not on fire," which is also a good place to start! Once I start listing things, unexpected connections and memories come up, sweetening the day and making me aware of that "something more" beyond myself. Sometimes we overcomplicate everything, even prayer. The great medieval mystic Meister Eckehart advised us that if all we can say is "Thank you," then we have said enough.

Even as statistics show that people aren't engaged in organized religion, we still maintain rituals that feed our souls. Journaling is a wonderful way to practice gratitude prayer, and there have never been more journals and gratitude notebooks in our bookstores. Perhaps you already have a gratitude practice at the end of the day, listing three things that you're grateful for, either by writing them down or sharing with your family around the dinner table, or with your partner before falling asleep. I struggle to maintain that daily practice, so instead I take out my journal on a tech sabbath day and try to fill a few pages with reflections and memories that have brought me joy. And as Brené Brown affirms in her book *Braving the Wilderness*, the key to joy is practicing gratitude.

Sometimes people worry about gratitude seeming selfish or self-involved, as others have so little. Brown argues the opposite: "When you are grateful for what you have, I know you understand the magnitude of what I have lost." Her research also revealed that "when we surrender our own joy to make those in pain feel less alone or to make ourselves feel less guilty or seem more committed, we deplete ourselves of what it takes to feel fully alive and fueled by purpose." Gratitude isn't just for yourself, ironically. Being grateful actually helps us show up for others.

It won't surprise you that recent research suggests that gratitude improves our mental well-being, too. Numerous studies over the past decade have found that people who consciously count their blessings tend to be happier and less depressed. But it's important to note the two key elements of a gratitude practice.

Robert Emmons, professor of psychology at the University of California, Davis, explains in an essay for the Greater Good Science Center magazine that gratitude is an affirmation of goodness: "We affirm that there are good things in the world, gifts and benefits we've received." The crucial second half of the practice is about recognizing "the sources of this goodness as outside of ourselves. . . . We acknowledge that other people—or even higher powers, if you're of a spiritual mindset—gave us many gifts, big and small, to help us achieve the goodness in our lives."

Giving thanks to that source of goodness outside ourselves—whether a specific person, the luck of a certain opportunity, or something more deeply spiritual—contributes to reorienting our lives away from the dominant cultural narrative of our own successes, desires, and ambitions and toward a perspective that is more holistic. "Gratitude is not about stuff," explains author and scholar of American religion and culture Diana Butler Bass in her book *Grateful*. "Gratitude is the emotional response to the surprise of our very existence, to sensing that inner light and realizing the astonishing sacred, social, and scientific events that brought each one of us into being."

Prayers of thanksgiving are not meant to tidy over the messiness of our lives, however. Bass writes, "Gratitude is not a psychological or political panacea, like a secular prosperity gospel, one that denies pain or overlooks injustice, because being grateful does not 'fix' anything. Pain, suffering, and injustice—these things are all real. They do not go away." What gratitude does, however, is dispel the idea that this is all that life offers, that despair wins the day. "Gratitude gives us a new story. It opens our eyes to see that every life is, in unique and dignified ways, graced: the lives of the poor, the castoffs, the sick, the jailed, the exiles, the abused, the forgotten as well as those in more comfortable physical circumstances. Your life. My life. We all share in the ultimate gift—life itself. Together. Right now."

A very powerful way to come into that precious awareness is to practice the memento mori, the reminder that we, too, shall die. Similar versions of this practice show up in classical antiquity, in Japanese samurai culture, in Tibetan Buddhism, and in the Mexican festival of the Day of the Dead. Hugely popular in early modern Europe, the practice instructed people to shift their attention from earthly things and raise their longings to the eternal instead. With much shorter lifespans and the threat of the plague always near, our historical counterparts were confronted with the reality of death early and often. Artists like Frans Hals started to work symbols of death into their still-life paintings or family scenes: nearly always there's a skull hidden in the corner or left on a desk, for example. A memento mori practice is like a camera lens that zooms out. Remembering that we'll die, and confronting the reality that it might be today, helps us see our lives with greater perspective. The problems we've been paying such close attention to and worrying about don't disappear, but they do fade into a broader background. Most likely we all have practiced the memento mori, perhaps unknowingly, when we go to a loved one's funeral or walk past a graveyard. Often, we'll feel it most when a young person is killed in an accident, for example. We become painfully aware of the brevity of life.

To integrate this practice, find a place where you won't be interrupted for a little while. Imagine you only have a year left to live. What might you do with the time you have left? Spend some time thinking or journaling. Visualize where you might go, who you'd want to talk to. What you'd stop doing. Now imagine you only have a week. How might you choose to spend your last days? What would your last meal be? Who would you be with? Now imagine it is your last hour alive. And then your last minute. Your last breath. This very breath you're breathing right now.

Without knowing it, I had been practicing something very similar when I was recovering from a serious accident in which I broke both my lower legs and a wrist and double-fractured my spine. As I fell from the pier in Scotland onto the rocks twenty feet below, I remember thinking, "Aha. So this is how it ends." I'd been walking along the pier with friends and had climbed up to a narrow pathway with the sea to my right. We were singing songs from the musical *Grease*, and as I enthusiastically shouted "shoobop sha wadda wadda yippity boom de boom!", I hopped forward—or at least what I thought was forward. But because I was looking to my left, in fact I had jumped straight off the side, to the right, falling onto the rocks as the tide was out. Even as I type this my hands are sweating, over a decade later! So, as I slowly recovered, once my casts came off and I could gently rotate my ankles, I started to say every morning, "I might die today." Once I was able to shower, I used the morning habit of washing to practice this ritual. I'd let the hot water run over my body while I meditated on the people I loved and the real possibility that this might well be my last day alive. "I might die today."

I had created a memento mori: a reflection on my mortality.

There are many ways to adapt this practice. My friend Darrell Jones III has built it into his workout. You might download an app like WeCroak, which pings you five times a day to remind you of your coming death. Or you can find a short phrase to say out loud as you put on moisturizer or makeup in the morning, or every time you get in the car. The secret is to repeat it often, so that you experience a regular moment of reflection and gratitude for being alive.

SUPPLICATION

The final stage of this prayer sequence is supplication, in which we mindfully hold someone or something in the presence of the divine. Of the four stages, this one comes closest to what I always thought prayer was—the holy shopping list of wants and needs. But really, it's a chance to hold the people we love in our compassionate awareness. We can create a small list of people we want to wish well, or focus on those who might be lonely or sick or depressed. And of course, this is where we can set intentions for ourselves also. I love to follow Jack Kornfield's Buddhist metta (loving-kindness) meditation practice, where we repeat three intentions over and over again. We start with ourselves, then turn to someone we love, then to a stranger, and then to someone with whom we are struggling:

> *May I be safe and free from suffering.*
> *May I be as happy and healthy as it is possible for me*
>   *to be.*
> *May I have ease of being.*

> *May [she] be safe and free from suffering.*
> *May [she] be as happy and healthy as it is possible*
>   *for [her] to be.*
> *May [she] have ease of being.*

By saying them over and over, we form a rhythm to our supplication prayers. I have been amazed that—on some days—it is absolutely possible to be angry and frustrated with someone and still be able to practice this kind of loving intention toward them. Prayer is like a workshop for the soul. In it, we get to work out all the kinks and knots of life. It can soften resentment and make space for forgiveness. What we do might not magically change other people or the world outside, but prayer certainly changes us.

Supplication can look like intentional well-wishing, but it can also simply be the process by which we lift up the things in life we need help with. We call into our conscious mind the fears we might have, for example. Sometimes I create a list in my journal, trying to fill the whole page to ensure I am digging deep enough to clear out all the gunk in my mind. "I'm afraid I'm going to fail this exam. I'm afraid I'm going to put on weight. I'm afraid I've made the wrong choice moving to the other side of the world. I'm afraid I won't love myself fully. I'm afraid I said the wrong thing to so-and-so." On and on, just listing whatever comes into my head. Writing it down or saying it out loud seems to take the sting out of things that are haunting me. That is the power of supplicatory prayer. It creates a place for fear and simultaneously puts fear in its place. It allows us to say what scares us without allowing it to overwhelm us. A spaciousness appears, a bigger perspective on our suffering. Maybe our timeline lengthens, seeing this moment in the context of a much longer history, or our individual perspective widens so that we're considering the interests of other living things besides ourselves. Yet the listing-fears prayer sometimes felt incomplete somehow. I'd speak the fears aloud in the shower, the fears mingling with the steam and just floating around the bathroom. So, on a whim, I started to sing a song I'd learned from my sisters, which has very simple lyrics:

Kindle the flame
To lighten the dark
And take all fear away.

Here was a way to transform the fears! Not that I felt some deity swoop in and clear the deck, but a simple way to bring "primary speech" to my awareness and then offer these truths up with a little song. I'd repeat it until I felt complete. Needless to say, those issues wouldn't be magically solved by the time I was finished—but my relationship to my fears was different. I was calmer, more compassionate with myself. Simply singing to myself in this small ritual allowed me to remember that, ultimately, whatever trials I was experiencing, these too would pass.

Zen Buddhist teacher and writer Cheri Huber takes this practice one step further. She explains how you can use your phone to record yourself speaking aloud all your fears, pains, and angers—describing all the frustrations you feel in great detail. Then, after taking a short break, listen to the recording, as if hearing someone else's problems, and bring to them the kind of compassion and love that you would to a friend or stranger. After listening through loving ears, record a loving message back to yourself with some words of wisdom and care. Then, after another break, listen to that second message.

Perhaps my favorite way to offer prayers of supplication is through the art of blessing. Blessings are rare for most of us today, and yet human life was once saturated with blessings. We might have been blessed before setting off on a journey, at the start of a meal, before getting married, or at the arrival of Shab-bat. "With the demise of religion, many people are left stranded in a chasm of emptiness and doubt; without rituals to recognize, celebrate, or negotiate the vital thresholds of people's lives," writes John O'Donohue in his book *To Bless the Space Between Us.* "This is where we need to retrieve and reawaken our capacity for blessing. If we approach our decisive thresholds with reverence and attention, the crossing will bring us more than we could ever have hoped for. This is where blessing invokes and awakens every gift the crossing has to offer." No longer are the threshold moments a time for fear. Transitions become the way in which our lives find rhythm, depth, and meaning.

Inspired by O'Donohue's essay, podcast cohost Vanessa Zoltan and I have blessed a character in the Harry Potter books at the end of every episode since we started in 2016. Of course, the blessing is for a fictional literary figure, but nevertheless, we offer an invitation for the listener to receive the blessing for themselves also. Importantly, a blessing doesn't erase what makes life difficult, but it does reach deeply into life to draw out the hidden fruit of suffering. And if there is no fruit at all, we can at least be present to that emptiness. Through blessing, we can transform an isolating or painful experience into something that at very least is no longer alone.

To bless, we don't just share a thought. Blessing is about digging deeper and speaking from the soul. We reach into the depths of our being and speak from the unalterable wholeness that is always at our center. Meister Eckehart identified that place within us as a place that neither time nor space could touch. In middle high German, he called it the *"vunklein"*: the simple, divine sparklet within us. Sometimes in blessing, Vanessa and I surprise ourselves with whom we choose and how we express ourselves. Because in some way the blessing is coming from beyond us, as much as it comes from within us.

A true blessing affirms two things. First, our blessings affirm our inherent wholeness. A blessing is never about developing ourselves or becoming more holy and enlightened. It is the gift of helping one another to remember our ever-present enough-ness. And second, our blessings affirm our inherent interconnectedness. A blessing is a practice of "discover[ing] and express[ing] those parts of ourselves that innately understand our connectedness," as writer David Spangler explains.

This is why receiving a blessing is not false positivity or cheap Instagram hashtaggery. Blessings are not about standing in front of a camera with ocean vistas or sunset skies glowing behind you. Blessings embrace what is most difficult in our life. Through the practice of blessing we honor life's pain with dignity and depth.

O'Donohue describes blessings as "a circle of light drawn around a person to protect, heal, and strengthen." In this, he drew on ancient Celtic spiritual practice. The Celts drew a *caim*—a circle—around themselves in times of danger. Whether or not they believed in magical powers, it reminded them that they were always surrounded by the divine, that the mystery of the holy encircles us and entwines through us wherever we are. Blessings exist to remind us of that fact. If we've gone out of tune, a blessing or prayer of supplication brings us back into harmony. That's why, for O'Donohue, a blessing has real power. We must offer it with conviction because "the beauty of blessing is its belief that it can affect what unfolds."

THE NECESSITY OF COMMUNITY

Let me offer a gentle warning here. Of all the experiences of connection, this last one—connecting to the transcendent—is both the most mystical and the most powerful. You meet some people whom you just know have that deep connection to something bigger. They radiate spiritual maturity. But as ever, with great power comes great responsibility. It is vital that we do not lose ourselves in these practices of prayer and sacred connection. We need others to keep us grounded, responsible, and safe. Too many stories from history tell of fanaticism and zealous ideologues who may have found a beautiful and powerful way of engaging the sacred—but have become obsessed that their way is the *only* way.

This is why we invite our listeners to send us voicemails for the podcast. Hearing other perspectives enriches our own sacred practice experience because it keeps our reading fresh and our thoughts sharp. We can more easily understand differing points of view and be held to account when we interpret a word or phrase in a way that unintentionally hurts others.

A community of fellow practitioners does not need to be large. Just a handful of fellow travelers can open new doors and widen our imaginations. When our commitment wanes and our conviction falters, a community can give us the oomph we need to keep going. As spiritual beginners, we're bound to falter and flail our way through our sacred practices. And even when we find a rhythm, new and unexpected challenges will arrive at our door. A community like this can take all sorts of shapes. Of course, a traditional congregation works for some. But others get together with a group of friends once a year to discuss their spiritual lives. You might have a buddy with whom you get on the phone once a month, or a scheduled time to go for a walk with your partner and talk about this.

I have learned that, at some point, finding a teacher or spiritual director who can tailor advice to take you further is not only necessary, but a relief! Even though they may be unknown to you now, there are guides out there who can help you navigate the human spirit. Until then, if you're ever in doubt about how you're engaging in sacred practice, simply remember the great African theologian Augustine of Hippo who instructed that if we're ever finding our awareness led away from the twofold love of the divine and our neighbor, then we have not fulfilled the purpose of the practice.

MAKING PRAYER YOUR OWN

I never thought I'd describe myself as someone who prays. Perhaps you are the same. And yet, using this frame of adoration, contrition, thanksgiving, and supplication, I've found a way to structure how I can connect with that which is greater than me.

You might have traditions that you were raised with that you can adapt and reinterpret. Or you might explore mixing together elements that bring alive a practice of prayer in a whole new way. I was very surprised to find myself repeating a traditional prayer in the midst of the snow boots and winter jackets in the closet of my old house. I'd learned it at my boarding school back in England, and I'd always resented knowing it by heart. It is the Lord's Prayer, a central element of Christian devotional life. The opening words in particular—"Our Father," the ultimate patriarchal language for god—felt bitter in my mouth. Surely, I said to myself, if god is a mystery, there has to be language that awakens my soul rather than flattens it. So drawing on my love of forests, I found a Tarot deck brimming with images set in woodlands. Now, when starting my adoration prayer time, I pull a card out of the deck, lay the card face up, and allow that day's image to spark my imagination of what the divine looks like: a wolf, the King of Stones, a wren, the Page of Arrows, or two twisting serpents symbolizing Balance. And so, I start the most traditional of prayers by saying, "Our Wolf, who art in Heaven" or "Our Balance, who art in Heaven." Whatever the cards offer stretches my image of what or who god might be that day!

Prayer can be enriched in a hundred ways. Even how we set up our space is an opportunity for creativity. Lighting candles or incense is a simple way to set the tone, or like me, you can wrap a throw around your shoulders as you enter prayer time. Of course, prayer shawls are used all over the world, and for good reason. They embody the embrace of the divine. Whenever I put on the purple yak-wool throw, given to me by my pilgrim buddy Caroline, I feel warmth, calm, and comfort, as if I can hide within it and yet be emboldened by it at the same time. There's nothing inherently special about the throw itself, but just like a sacred text, if I come back to it and wear it again and again, it becomes imbued with meaning and memory. Others might kiss their journal as the Torah scroll is kissed, or simply lift their pen and say, "Let me write with truth and love," before they start journaling. Whatever you do, if it helps bring your attention to this time of reflection, it is valuable and worth ritualizing.

If, after all this, prayer still sounds like an impossibility, too foreign or religious in some way, just start with this: Talk to yourself. Use those four stages as prompts to talk about your life, about what you've done and what you've failed to do. Talk about who you are and who you wish to become and who the people you love are (and the people you don't love, too). Talk about what matters most, even—and especially—if you know that nobody is listening except yourself. Because unless we are honest, unless we speak the truth, we will forget what we want to stay loyal to.

We have everything we need to start either bringing this practice into our lives or enriching existing rituals: the daily habits that we can add some words to. What can we tell ourselves while putting on our morning moisturizer or getting in the car? These are the micro-moments where we can return to our hearts and cling to them. Walter Burghardt, the noted Jesuit theologian, defined contemplative prayer as simply a "long loving look at the real." When we can be present to reality, when we can speak in that form of primal speech, we become most fully ourselves. This has supreme value to the world! What a gift to those around us that we might live our fullest lives. The decisions we make, how we spend our time and money, how we engage in politics—all are enriched when we can take a long loving look at the real.

If journaling doesn't float your boat, you can dance or sing your prayers, or bake or paint them. Knead all your love into the dough, or get a charcoal and a piece of paper and give form to the anger and sadness that is hanging over you. All that matters is that you use these embodied practices to connect with the truth going on inside you. Start a list of people you love and want to hold in your heart. Make notes in your gratitude journal, and do Morning Pages. Note down new things that happen in your life. Acknowledge the burdens you feel, the forces you can't control. Ask what you are afraid of. Where you feel stuck or joyful or a spark of curiosity.

Remember, there's no need to buy anything new or change how you're journaling. Just notice, do you often sit in a particular chair? Or make tea before you start? Is there a cushion or quilt that you rest your writing arm on? You can make each of these sacred by giving them a blessing or a kiss. Think of home organizer Marie Kondo, who has revealed the spirituality of tidying up: hold the item close to your chest, close your eyes, and offer it your heartfelt thanks. Every moment can be a moment of sacred connection, a chance for a sneaky prayer.

CHAPTER 5

Already Connected

I HOPE THIS BOOK has helped you see two things. First, that you already have a host of rituals we might call spiritual practices—even if you'd never use that language. Reading, walking, eating, resting, reflecting: these are legitimate and worthy of your attention and care, and they can be the foundation of a life of deep connection. Second, I hope you feel empowered to translate ancient traditions to enrich those modern practices and that you feel permission to be creative in combining the ancient and the emergent.*

We live in an age in which many of us have been pushed beyond our limits to work harder, perform better, earn more,

---

* I'm indebted to Alan Webb, Sarah Bradley, and the Alt*Div project for this phrase.

do more, and be more, where we are more medicated and depressed, more anxious and alone, than ever before. Younger
generations are drowning in debt, older generations struggle to retire when they want to, and we live amid the largest wealth disparities in American history and the crushing
weight of white supremacy. All the while, the breakneck speed
of change ushered in by the internet and consumer capitalism
is reshaping the entire spiritual and community landscape.
Nearly everyone I know feels as if they are falling short of
some predefined standard that is completely out of reach so
that our near-constant state of not feeling we are enough frustrates our enjoyment of moments that could and should be
meaningful. These structural inequities literally steal our joy.

This will not last. It cannot. Too many people are getting
wise to the trap into which we've been led. People are closing their Facebook accounts, building new solutions to direct
their own learning, and changing the structures of homeown-
ership to live cooperatively. In the midst of these age-defining
changes, the old answers, rituals, and structures that helped
us find meaning and connection no longer speak to our lived
experience.

In the midst of this, many of us are unbundling and remixing our spiritual lives and re-creating practices that help
us connect to ourselves, to one another, to nature, and to the
transcendent. It isn't always easy. But we have inherited great
traditions from our spiritual ancestors so that what we read,
who we eat with, how we travel, and when we take time to
reflect all have the potential to be transformed into a sacred

moment of connection—as do walking the dog, going for a swim, stepping into the shower, driving to work, and cooking dinner. Though we can invent entirely new stories and structures and new customs to follow, there are rich layers of meaning to be uncovered when we return to traditions and reimagine them for our own contexts. Drawing on the practices we were raised with or that have been taught to us, we have permission to claim that our embodiment of them is genuine, honorable, and worthy.

A RULE OF LIFE

What do we do once we've identified ways to deepen our connection to each of the four layers? How can we hold them together—even if we're drawing from different sources and inspirations in our life? Spiritual growth doesn't depend on doing *more* than the soul is probably already doing, but on doing the same things in a design instead of in a muddle. So there's one final tool to share, one that I'm noticing people unknowingly re-create in a multitude of ways (Holstee Reflection Cards, Gretchen Rubin's tracking worksheets, Alain de Botton's School of Life books, the Monk Manual, a friend's checklist on his bedroom wall for keeping track of his practices and commitments). This is the monastic practice of a Rule of Life.

A Rule of Life is a way of centering our commitment to a way of being and the rituals and practices that help us live our lives in this way. Practiced by monastic communities since the third and fourth centuries, it's a way of keeping a steady rhythm as we move through our lives. The word "rule" has little to do with behaviors that are permitted and forbidden; instead, it draws on the Latin meaning of its root word, *regula*, to regulate or guide. So you can think of this as a Pattern of Life, if that feels better. In Jewish tradition, the musar movement has a similar focus on offering a structure to help us become the people we want to be.

The idea is that we can create a living rhythm that holds us through our days. Usually practiced by communities, today more and more of us are creating our own personal Rules of Life, though we can live them together in pairs or large groups, of course. At their best, Rules of Life give us a way to join together the values and intentions we hold and the practices that help us live those intentions out. In other words, the rituals we explored throughout this book add up to something—well, someone—and a Rule of Life helps us structure that process.

Traditionally, a community Rule of Life might have more than thirty different principles or practices. Together, all these mini rules make up the full Rule of Life. These individual rules might cover how monks pray, eat, work, and live together, for example. Each morning, monastic communities would gather and read aloud a single rule from the shared text that makes up the Rule of Life. In so doing, they'd work through their entire Rule of Life over the course of a month or so. Reading aloud together would plant the seed to focus on that particular rule for the day. For instance, the forty-eighth rule of Saint

Benedict opens with "Idleness is the enemy of the soul. There-fore, the brothers [monks] should be occupied at set times in manual labor, and again at other set times in divine reading." There are hundreds of different communities with different rules. Saint Benedict's Rule is the most famous, but there are many others—the Rules of Saint Francis and Saint Clare, or the many newer rules written in the centuries since these early spiritual leaders. Often, they articulate a value and then illus-trate how that value might be lived out.

Putting your own Rule of Life together will take a little bit of time and some thoughtfulness, but it is entirely doable. First, think of a number of virtues or intentions that you want to live out. It could be as few as three or as many as thirty. When I put mine together, I chose to write a rule for each of the four connections in this book—to my inner self, to others, to the natural world, and to the transcendent.

Then, for each topic, write out a few notes and start to draft a few lines or up to half a page in length. To get started, you can draw on Charles LaFond's book *Note to Self: Creating Your Guide to a More Spiritual Life* or the little workbook by Brother David Vryhof called *Living Intentionally: A Workbook for Creating a Personal Rule of Life.*

I started by writing a rule to help me connect with myself. Knowing that I tend to overwork and escape into my email inbox when life gets hard (because at least then I am dealing with something that I can tangibly succeed in!), I know that rest and nonwork time are vital to my well-being. I started to practice my tech-free sabbath days in 2014, which has been my most important spiritual discipline. But the practice slips away when I'm traveling and away from home, when I suddenly have a big deadline, or when an important Leeds United soccer game is on. I need a north star, something that reminds me of why I started the practice, why it is important to me, to keep bringing me back to what I know truly matters. So I had a go at writing that down.

Rest is necessary.

Without it, pleasurable things become chores. Priorities fall out of sight, and I fall into destructive behavior patterns. Rest is a responsibility—to the work I care about and the people who look to me for leadership.

I will want to check one last email. To check off one last action.

If an unavoidable sabbath incursion appears—a wedding, a funeral, or another significant life moment—I will schedule an alternative day of rest.

I will not travel on a rest day. I will be home or at a restful place on a Friday night.

I will know if I honor this Rule when I turn down enjoyable, even lucrative, opportunities in order to keep my sabbath.

I will turn off my phone and my laptop at nightfall on Friday, and I will not turn them on again until dusk on Saturday. This is a sacred rhythm, to re-enter our living planet's regular pattern.

Sabbath is not a luxury. It is a right. Who am I to refuse it?

The sabbath incubates and unleashes my most creative ideas and is the birthplace of beautiful projects and desires, not because I force them, but because I can receive them.

In sabbath time, I can lay down my grasping nature and enjoy every breath. I sing. I draw. I write. I sleep. I walk. I eat. I talk. I listen. I am quiet. I ponder. I light a candle.

Temptations will only increase if I start to slip. Then, without fail, I'll hit a crisis as I start to burn out. Sabbath is here to help.

Of course, I fall short in keeping my tech sabbath all the time. We wouldn't need a rule if it were easy! But rereading this regularly helps me connect with the strength of my intention. It reminds me of what it feels like when I'm living in line with my commitments, when I have time to sing to myself, to stare out of the window and let new ideas arise, or to think of others who might appreciate being reached out to. If I'm able to graciously maneuver through unexpected life bumps, you can bet I've been keeping my tech sabbath. When I'm grouchy and tired, feeling resentful and isolated, I'm likely to have been overworking and not sticking with the practice.

It is helpful to think of living a rule for a set amount of time. You might start with a month or a particular season. If you're feeling confident, you can make the commitment to live it out for a year. But you should not expect enormous changes in relatively short timelines. As Rabbi Simcha Zissel Ziv, the Alter of Kelm, reminds us in Alan Morinis's book *Everyday Holiness*, the transformation of the human heart is "the work of a lifetime and that is just why you have been given a lifetime in which to do it."

As you start to put pen to paper, ask someone to look it over before you commit to living out your intentions. I've found myself sharing my rule with at least one wise person I trust to let me know if there's anything that I've written that concerns them. This practice will help you avoid falling into the shame trap where you berate yourself for not living up to who you want to be. Connecting with someone who has some experience accompanying people as they deepen their spiritual practices, like a spiritual director or an elder, can be a wonderful way of finding support.

As you read this book, you've been thinking of practices you already do or you've imagined ways that you might integrate ancient wisdom into daily habits. A Rule of Life can help you hold all of that together. In an era of disconnection, this can be your own personal knapsack of connection. A Rule of Life can reflect back to you the words that open your heart and lift your spirit, reminding you of your inherent connection to yourself, other people, the natural world, and the great mystery of being alive.

A Practice Isn't a Practice Without Commitment

At this point, we can no longer escape the frustrating reality that to deepen a habit—whether it's taking a break from tech or deciding to eat together—we must commit with some amount of rigor. A spiritual practice should feel more like working out than going shopping or a having a luxury spa date. When embarking on a practice—whether basketball or poetry—its efficacy in connecting us with what matters most depends on our dependability. Unfortunately, that means that only practicing when we feel like it defeats the purpose because the times when we least want to sit down on the meditation cushion or pick up a pen are exactly when we need it most! The Dalai Lama famously explains that although he usually meditates for an hour a day, on a particularly busy day he makes sure to meditate for two.

To be clear, this is hard. I'm famous in my family for starting things but not finishing them. Yet the results with spiritual disciplines take time. There are no medal ceremonies or honors classes for those who excel. Indeed, the most spiritually mature people I've met are the least well known.

To set yourself up for success, I've found making a time-limited commitment is a helpful first step. If I know I am committed for eight weeks, or seven days, or twenty minutes, that helps me make it through the hardest moments of the practice. As a spiritual beginner, I've found it affirming to read Gretchen Rubin explain in her book *The Happiness Project* that of all the new tricks she's tried to help her live a happier life, putting a list of daily commitments on the wall and ticking them off as she went along was the most powerful. There's no shame in this. Novices—new monks or nuns—entering a monastery would recognize this kind of discipline and tracking of data. It's simply how we need to begin.

In hard times when we're trying to stick with a practice—meditating, say, or trying to send waves of love and compassion to a stranger on the bus every morning—think of the practice like an old friend. Sometimes the hours together are stimulating and inspiring. We feel understood, cared for, and seen. But other times, hanging out can feel a little dull. Perhaps we're tired. Or we've had a bad day. A true old friend will stick with us even during the fallow times, when our connection doesn't feel enriching or fruitful. But because we care for one another, and we know that there'll be a time in the future where the delight of continued accompaniment through life outshines the meager times, we stay committed to each other.

And just like exploring new rituals and making up traditions can be fun and creative, it is the oldest and oft-repeated practices that hold the most meaning in the end. In a world where we're constantly treated as consumers instead of citizens, where the only way we're invited to engage with the world is by buying it, we ought to be suspicious of always chasing the latest trend. Instead of acting like spiritual tourists, skimming the frothy fun off the surface, let's drink more deeply and luxuriate in the hidden delights of the real nourishment beneath. Like a cocktail, the good stuff is at the bottom!

This doesn't mean we can't have beautiful and transcendent one-off experiences! These moments are precious, but they do not a practice make. A practice must be repeated over time. Often when we start something new we experience the joys of novelty. Perhaps we have beginners' luck or simply enjoy telling others about this thing that we're trying. Either way, don't be surprised when, at some point, the practice starts to lose its initial sheen. Repeating a practice over and over again requires internal discipline, especially when the going gets tough or we're tired or we don't feel like it. So hang in there. After all, what we practice, we become.

As we've recorded over two hundred episodes of *Harry Potter and the Sacred Text*, I've been astounded at the sheer pleasure of sticking with something for so long! Even though we come back to the same story, with the same characters, with the same practices every week, still there are new discoveries to be made. So many listeners have written to us saying that they never thought there would be new angles to the wizarding world that they hadn't yet discovered or discussed after countless rereads and Tumblr threads. Yet because our own ever-changing lives keep being mirrored in the text, there are always new ideas to be revealed. Certain words or phrases that we've studied closely now hang heavy with meaning. Rereading them reminds me of my friendship with Vanessa in specific moments, recalling memories of who I was and connecting it to who I have become. So whatever your connection practices become, once you've found something that feels right, stick with it. It is the surest way forward.

The Tensions, Ambiguities, and Mysteries

In many ways, our understanding of "religion" over the last few hundred years is an anomaly. Because the West has been deeply marked by a Protestant Christian understanding, we assume religion is all about what you believe. That's part of it, of course, but most of the rest of the world—and certainly most of history—points to a different way of thinking about religion: that it's about what you practice.

Classicist Sally Humphreys has written extensively about religion in ancient Greece, for example. She argues that the Greeks didn't think of themselves as having a religion per se. They honored specific gods on Mount Olympus but also river nymphs and abstract ideas such as Wisdom and Victory. They called forth these great powers through a variety of practices, including blood sacrifice, pouring libations, and consulting oracles. They prayed for, cursed, and blessed one another. When war or trade brought Greeks into relationship with other nations or cultures, they simply included those new gods in their own sacred world. Ralph Anderson explains in *The Oxford Handbook of Ancient Greek Religion* that gods honored by the Greeks came from Thrace, Egypt, Syria, and Phrygia, among others. This sprawl of gods was never understood as a unified heavenly tableau. There simply wasn't what scholars call a systematic theology: a complete and logical rationale of how everything fits together.

And frankly, I think that's how most people actually live their lives—religious or not. Most of us are made of a mix of cultural assumptions, childhood traditions, peak experiences, deep worries and shames, secret hopes and desires, unexplained intuitions, and radically wonderful ideas. We can think one thing in the morning and another in the afternoon. And who knows what we believe at 3 a.m. when we get an unexpected call from the emergency room. Like the ancient Greeks, we don't have complete answers on why we do some practices. Walk into any congregation and ask the members why they do a shared ritual and you'll get as many answers as there are people. Probably more. Spirituality and religion always deal with tensions, ambiguities, and mysteries. To some extent, that's what they are there for.

While training to become a minister, my teacher Stephanie Paulsell suggested to her mentor that she wasn't ready to celebrate the Eucharist, Christianity's most important ritual. "I don't really know what it means yet," she explained. Her mentor smiled and replied, "Stephanie, we don't eat the bread and wine because we know what it means. We do it because we are learning what it means." At their heart, rituals like the Eucharist help us live in a great paradox, one that has run throughout this book that we've not yet named. But now it's time.

BUILDING, GROWING, AND REMEMBERING

As we live out our longing by setting intentions and engaging our practices of deep connection, it can start to feel like another item on the to-do list. Even the language we use seems to support that notion. For example, we talk often of "building community" or "making connections." It sounds like work, and in a way this makes sense. It takes real effort to create the conditions in which we feel connected—especially today, when so many of us feel isolated from one another and the world around us. Building community and making connections suggest the need for heavy lifting, specialized skills, and planning tools. But nurturing a lifestyle that acknowledges the soul, that makes space for connection, and that heals isolation can be reframed to be less about work and more about organic growth.

I learned this concept in the context of "growing community," a term I picked up from my colleague Angie Thurston when we started our *How We Gather* research. Knowing that relationships of all kinds interact more like natural ecosystems than machines, it is helpful to look to nature-based metaphors to understand how human connection deepens. Yet it goes beyond just growing community; it applies to each of the four levels of connection in this book. We don't manufacture connection. It grows, like a tree, with time. Though we have tried to mechanize the processes of reflection and meeting people with a plethora of apps—think of speed-dating and meditation apps with gamified incentives—these nearly always feel forced, like roses in wintertime. How we connect to ourselves, one another, the world around us, and the divine goes through seasons, just like the rhythm of the earth. Sometimes there's a bleak numbness to how we feel about our connectedness. Sometimes it feels like we're spending a lot of time planting seeds, but little reward is blossoming yet. Other times, we're overwhelmed by the bounty of love and joy we experience, like an orchard laden with summer fruit. Just like the land, we too will plant, harvest, and lie fallow now and then.

But even more striking than that metaphor of growth is how John O'Donohue invites us to think about connection.

In a conversation with Buddhist teacher Sharon Salzberg recorded in 1998, he explained, "I can't believe in any of this stuff about creating community. I think the whole project of trying to build community is misplaced. I think community *is*. It is ontologically there. So, the project is more about awakening." For him, connection is remembered, or revealed, because we are already "dangerously involved with each other in an incredibly intimate but unseen way." That's what it means to be human. Connection just is. We are each connected to every other thing.

This essential truth is written all over our *How We Gather* work. If that research proved anything, it's that connection isn't outdated or lost; it is happening all around and among us. Many of the most effective leaders we got to know through our research had been raised in vibrant communities. Many were children of ministers, rabbis, and summer camp directors. The experience of being in community had seeped into their bones. And their contemporary expressions of community were created by remembering what it felt like to be deeply connected.

Connection, for O'Donohue, is about love awakening in our lives. "In the night of your heart, it is like the dawn breaking within you. Where before there was anonymity, now there is intimacy; where before there was fear, now there is courage," he writes in his classic *Anam Cara*. All of us need to be reminded, often multiple times a day, that we are inherently worthy of those deep and holy links and that—no matter what we do—we are intrinsically connected.

And yet there are days, sometimes weeks and months, when that feels simply untrue. In those times, all we can feel is our loneliness. Not just from other people, but a profound distance from ourselves or an absence of the greater meaning and purpose that we might other times feel. As theologian Paul Tillich wrote, "Existence is separation!"

And here is the paradoxical secret: connection and isolation are bound to each other.

I am confident that without my experience as a lonely closeted teenager at a boys' boarding school, I wouldn't be as passionate about deep connection today. We simply cannot know connection without also experiencing disconnection. There is nothing wrong with you when you feel that vast emptiness. Nothing you need to change. Nothing to fix. But there is one thing to do.

Remember.

Remember that both are true. The vast emptiness and the eternal connection. The sense of total aloneness and the interdependent belovedness. It is the paradox in which we live. And all of the practices and stories and strategies that we've explored in this book are simply there to help you, in moments of joy and sadness, overwhelm and barrenness, to remember.

ACKNOWLEDGMENTS

I am confident that without the tens of thousands of dedicated *Harry Potter and the Sacred Text* listeners, this book would not have found its way to print. Thank you to every single person who tunes in, letting Vanessa, Ariana, and me into your lives every week! I promise I'll bake a cake before we've finished *Deathly Hallows*. . . .

As for my partners in mischief, huge thanks to Ariana Nedelman's countless hours of editing and, now and then, laughing at my silly jokes. And a lifetime of thanks to Vanessa Zoltan for co-creating something magical—even when it seemed to the world that we were ridiculous. More than that, though, thank you for being an astonishingly good friend.

Thank you to my literary agent, Lisa DiMona. I look forward to many more Parisian lunches! Thanks also to Lauren Carsley and the Writers House team for their support.

Enormous thanks to my editor at HarperOne, Anna

Paustenbach. Your acute and thoughtful editing have brought clarity and impact far beyond my own capacity! Thank you also for your kindness throughout. I'll never forget your hilarious note in response to my first "vomit" draft. . . .

Thanks also to the whole HarperOne team, especially Mary Grangeia, Mickey Maudlin, Laina Adler, Judith Curr, Melinda Mullin, Julia Kent, Kathryn Hamilton, Gideon Weil, Aidan Mahony, and everyone who helped bring the book to life.

A deep bow of thanks to Dacher Keltner for generously writing the preface and his decades of research compiling the scientific evidence for so many of the practices that I describe in the book. Few people marry science and soulfulness with such skill, and Dacher is living proof of what beauty it creates!

To the Brothers of the Society of Saint John the Evangelist, thank you for your hospitality and generosity during my many writing visits to the quiet beauty of Emery House.

Thank you to the entire team at the Fetzer Institute, especially Michelle Scheidt and Bob Boisture, for supporting my work over the last four years. Michelle, thank you for your friendship and passion and for showing us where to find the best breakfast in Kalamazoo!

Without six wonderful years at Harvard Divinity School I'd never have known about most of the practices in this book. I am forever indebted to Dudley Rose for his capacity to find ways to make the magic happen, to Matthew Potts for his rigor and imagination, to Mark Jordan for his example and generous feedback, to David Hempton for saying yes, and to all my classmates and professors who have shown such generosity in teaching me. A special word of thanks to two torchbearers who have forever deepened and enlivened my spiritual and intellectual life. First, to Kerry Maloney, thank you for hearing me into speech and always, always offering a Word. I keep discovering how much I've learned from you without your ever formally being my teacher. And of course, to Stephanie Paulsell, thank you for showing me how to translate the beauty of tradition and for giving me the confidence to explore my own spiritual life with your steady arm at my back and encouraging words in my ear. You have given me endless riches!

A heartfelt thank-you to mentors, teachers, and elders old, new, and from a distance. Seth Godin, Erik Martínez Resly, Ken Beldon, Burns Stanfield, Nancy Ammerman, Jeff Lee, Gil Rendle, John Dorhauer, Carol Zinn, Neil Hamilton, Sue Mosteller, John O'Donohue, Nadia Bolz-Weber, Richard Holloway, Kai Grünewald, Solitaire Townsend, Brené Brown, Derek van Bever, Richard Parker, Kathleen McTigue, John Green, Richard Rohr, Abraham Joshua Heschel, Henri Nouwen, Parker Palmer, and especially Charlotte Millar for reopening the door to a spiritual life all the way back in London.

As I get older, I'm learning that life is about the people you meet and the things you create with them. Thanks to each of these co-travelers and co-creators for their friendship along the way: Hilary Allen, Caroline Howe, Jonathan Krones, Ariel Friedman, Jamie Henn, Morissa Sobelson Henn, Ingrid Warner, Mila Majic, Daniel Vockins, Marisa Egerstrom, Nicholas Hayes, Erika Carlsen, Andrew Bradley, Titiaan Palazzi, Lawrence Barriner II, Adam Horowitz, Lennon Flowers, Alan Webb, Sarah Bradley, Julianne Holt-Lunstad, Jen Bailey, Liliana Maria Percy Ruíz, Yoav Schlesinger, Sid Schwarz, Alex Evans, Aden van Noppen, Lisa Greenwood, Melissa Bartholomew Wood, Elan Babchuk, Sara Luria, Channon Ross, Amichai Lau-Lavie, Priya Parker, Tara-Nicholle Nelson, May Boeve, Michael Poffenberger, Broderick Greer, Timbo Shriver, Johnny Chatterton, Scott Perlo, Alex Smith, Mike Webb, Barry Finestone, Christian Peele, Julie Rice, Elizabeth Cutler, Danya Shults, Scott Heiferman, Jeff Walker, Vivek Murthy, and Jane Shaw, among many others.

Thanks also to the brave souls who read early drafts of the manuscript and offered insightful, kind, and suitably challenging feedback—especially Lawrence Barriner II, Hilary Allen, Andrew Bradley, Hanna Thomas, and Olivia Haughton Willis. (Liv—you, in particular, saw things on a page no one should have to read and still championed the project, for which I am forever grateful!) Thanks to Rachel Hills and Jieun Beck for sharing key insights on the book publishing process, to Maya Dusenbery for her precise fact-checking, and to Margie Dillenburg, Erica Williams Simon, Jeremy Heimans, and Natalya Sverjensky for their strategizing.

So many of the experiences that shaped this book I have had alongside my sister-in-work Angie Thurston. Whether speaking in front of a room of Methodist bishops, watching a man land in a field wearing a jetpack, or traveling through Otherworld, I love learning from, and shaping, the world with you. Who can say if I've been changed for the better? One hundred percent I can! To Angie, and to our third sibling-in-work,

Sue Phillips, I am forever indebted. Any spiritual deepening this book can encourage is wholly thanks to your friendship and example. Wouldn't be here without you!

To my family—Suzanne Hillen, Marc ter Kuile, Laura ter Kuile, Fleur ter Kuile, Rosa ter Kuile: I love you! I was once told that everyone's first book is about their mother. And this one is certainly no different. How my mother raised me, and nurtured our entire family, is woven into everything I've been able to share here. From the long walks through the Ashdown Forest, the VJK songs around the campfire, card games on Saturday night, you are really the author of this story.

And finally, thank you to my beloved husband Sean Lair. Right now, you're soaking orange-peel and baking fruit cake for our black-tie Christmas carol sing-a-long party next weekend. Thanks for putting up with my writing-vulnerability hangovers and always being my champion and copilot. I'm so glad we're together.